ARCHAEOLOGY AT THE SITE OF

THE MUSEUM OF THE AMERICAN REVOLUTION

T0097827

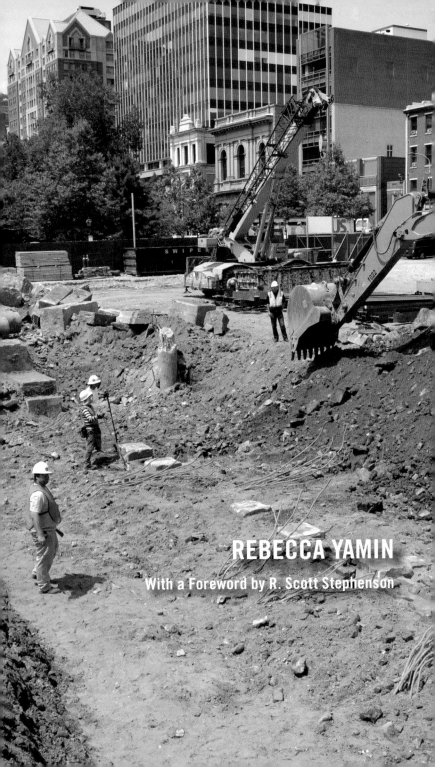

REBECCA YAMIN

With a Foreword by R. Scott Stephenson

ARCHAEOLOGY AT THE SITE OF THE MUSEUM OF THE AMERICAN REVOLUTION

A Tale of Two Taverns and the Growth of Philadelphia

TEMPLE UNIVERSITY PRESS
Philadelphia | Rome | Tokyo

Temple University Press
Philadelphia, Pennsylvania 19122
www.temple.edu/tempress

Design by Kate Nichols

Library of Congress Cataloging-in-Publication Data

Names: Yamin, Rebecca, 1942- author. | Stephenson, R. Scott, writer of
    foreword.
Title: Archaeology at the site of the Museum of the American
    Revolution : a tale of two taverns and the growth of Philadelphia /
    Rebecca Yamin ; with a foreword by R. Scott Stephenson.
Description: Philadelphia : Temple University Press, 2019. | Includes
    bibliographical references and index.
Identifiers: LCCN 2018023749 | ISBN 9781439916421 (paperback : alk.
    paper)
Subjects: LCSH: Philadelphia (Pa.)—Antiquities. | Museum of the
    American
    Revolution. | Excavations (Archaeology)—Pennsylvania—Philadelphia. |
    Historic sites–Pennsylvania–Philadelphia. | Urban
    archaeology–Pennsylvania–Philadelphia. | Archaeology and
    history—Pennsylvania—Philadelphia. | Philadelphia (Pa.)—History. |
    Philadelphia (Pa.)—Social life and customs.
Classification: LCC F158.3.Y36 2019 | DDC 974.8/1101—dc23 LC
    record available at https://lccn.loc.gov/2018023749

Printed in the United States of America

9 8 7 6 5 4 3 2 1

CONTENTS

ILLUSTRATIONS

FOREWORD

THE CONSTRUCTION of the Museum of the American Revolution began with one of the largest urban archaeology projects in Old City Philadelphia since the National Constitution Center was built nearly twenty years earlier. As a historian who has spent time "in the trenches" excavating at places like Monticello and Yorktown, it is hard to exaggerate how excited I was when demolition began on the old National Park Service Visitor Center at Third and Chestnut Streets. Having spent years building the creative team that developed the exhibit concepts for the new museum, I was hopeful that archaeology would reveal new stories about our neighborhood and objects that would provide tangible links to the nation's founding era.

On the eve of the American Revolution, the site of the Museum of the American Revolution sat near the center of the largest city in British North America, which was also one of the largest cities in the British Empire. Philadelphia's bustling, multiethnic, multilingual population drew from the peoples of Europe, Africa, and the Americas. Their material world of buildings, furnishings, fashions, and food reflected far flung lands connected by British merchant ships that plied the world's oceans. Those ships carried ideas as well as things, on printed pages and imprinted in minds. Thus, wrapped in a dressing gown made of brightly printed fabric from the Indian subcontinent, a Philadelphia merchant poring over ledgers bound in leather from Russia might have contemplated British parliamentary taxation as he sipped a strong punch made from rum, sugar, citrus, and spices gathered from three continents and served in a fine ceramic bowl from China.

In fact, it was a ceramic punch bowl from England, rather than China, that gave us our first electrifying glimpse of the coming of the American Revolution for the people living on and around the future site of our museum. Just a few weeks after the archaeological fieldwork began, I stopped by to chat with the crew and see what the excavation was revealing. On the site's southeast corner, the circular outlines of two brick-lined privies (or outhouses) had been carefully exposed by the heavy machinery operator, and the crew was preparing to excavate material from the first one. The rich, dark soil that filled the old privy was flecked with light colored shards of porcelain, creamware and stoneware vessels, the broken remains of mugs and cups, plates and saucers. Broken eighteenth-century bottle glass, bone, and other objects protruded from the fill. This is the kind of feature that stirs the heart of every archaeologist, including those like me who have not worked "in the dirt" for years.

It was August 19, 2014. It was my birthday. So I asked field director Tim Mancl, who supervised the crew of archaeologists on the site, for a present. "That looks like a promising feature," I observed, as they began carefully removing soil from the privy. "Please find me a 'No Stamp Act' teapot," I said. Everyone laughed. For students of the Revolutionary era, there is scarcely a more iconic object representing American resistance to British taxation than a handful of precious surviving English creamware teapots bearing the slogan No Stamp Act. Produced around 1765–1766 for export to the American colonies, these political objects are prized by the institutions that possess them—including Colonial Williamsburg, the Metropolitan Museum of Art, the National Museum of American History (Smithsonian), and the Peabody-Essex Museum. For a new national museum dedicated to exploring the history and legacies of the American Revolution, my bucket list definitely included and (spoiler alert) still includes a No Stamp Act teapot.

Just a few hours after I left the site and returned to our collection warehouse west of Philadelphia, Tim began texting me images from the field. Fragments of whitish English delftware were coming out of the brick-lined privy. When fit loosely together, the first handful of pieces revealed the painted decoration of a double-masted merchant ship in full sail and flying British flags. The words *Success to the Triphena* were visible below, and when the pieces were eventually fit together in the lab, we were electrified to find a nearly complete punch bowl made in Liverpool, England, in the early 1760s. The Triphena bowl, as it came to be known (although I still refer to it as my birthday present), turned out to have a direct connection to the Stamp Act Crisis and the beginnings of the colonial resistance movement that sparked a revolution.

That was just the beginning of the story. Feature 16, as the brick-lined privy (just one of many found by archaeologists on the museum site) was known, proved to be a remarkable time capsule that offered a rich and exciting glimpse of Revolutionary Philadelphia through the material lives of a family, their neighbors, and customers working and playing in and around a little back-alley tavern just a few minutes' walk from Independence Hall.

Rebecca Yamin's stirring account of the archaeological investigation of the Museum of the American Revolution site shows us what we lose when we fail to invest the time and resources to document and recover the irreplaceable records of human experience that lie beneath the streets and basements of twenty-first-century Philadelphia. The remains of the eighteenth-century world out of which arose one of the most important events in human history, the American Revolution, lie beneath our feet. We have only scratched the surface.

DR. R. SCOTT STEPHENSON

Vice President of Collections, Exhibitions and Programs
Museum of the American Revolution

ACKNOWLEDGMENTS

HISTORICAL ARCHAEOLOGY is a team effort. I was what we call the principal investigator for the archaeological excavation and analysis of the Museum of the American Revolution site, but I had lots of help. I am grateful to Matthew Harris, Douglas McVarish, and Grace Ziesing for the excellent work they did on the initial historical background study for the site in 2010. That study provided the framework for understanding what we found in the ground in 2014. Tim Mancl expertly oversaw daily field activities, single-handedly excavated the brick-lined well uncovered in the middle of the site, and brought his experience as an industrial archaeologist to the analysis of the remains left by the Lippincott Button Factory. He also put together an excellent field crew—Tod Benedict, Kathryn Wood, Kevin Bradley, Meagan Ratini, Katherine McCormick, T. Patrick Snyder, and Alexandra Vanko—all of whom did very good archaeology under not very easy circumstances. Huge cranes swirled around their heads and drills pounded in their ears. Tod and Kathryn occasionally took over supervisory roles and contributed significantly to the final report, Tod to the primary documentary research and Kathryn to ceramic analysis. Kevin did most of the in-field mapping, and he and Meagan completed a map study of changes over time.

Besides being a team effort, urban archaeology is collaborative. We could not have accomplished as much as we did without the assistance of D'Angelo Brothers, the contractor for the construction of the museum, and INTECH, the construction manager. The key to making it all work, however, was John McDevitt, the Museum of the American Revolution's director of design and construction. He ensured that we all accommodated each other's needs to the degree necessary and kept smiling in the process. I am enormously grateful to his ability to coordinate the many different activities and people it took to get the archaeological investigation done while construction was underway. John's support and the support of other museum personnel made all the difficulties worthwhile. That Scott Stephenson, the museum's director of collections and interpretation (now vice president of collections, exhibitions, and programming), had done archaeology in his past was particularly valuable. I am grateful for his interest in the work and am honored that he wanted to write the foreword to this book. ZeeAnn Mason, the museum's chief operating officer, has been working toward the creation of a museum of the American Revolution since the late 1990s, and, when the museum was planned for Valley Forge, I worked with John Milner Associates on an archaeological study of that site. It was a pleasure to work with ZeeAnn then, and I am grateful that she kept me in mind for the study of the museum's final site in Old City, Philadelphia. It is surely one of the best projects of my career. Credit is also due to Jed Levin, chief of the history branch for Independence National Historical Park. Jed oversaw the compliance required by the transfer of land from the Park Service to the Museum of the American Revolution and, as always, helped solve problems in the field and commented productively on our technical report.

Sara Jo Cohen, editor at Temple University Press, invited me to write this book. She had heard about the project through the press and thought it might work as a book. It is flattering, of course, to be asked to write a book and reassuring to know that archaeology, even archaeology done close to home, continues to interest the public. Archaeologists are famous for writing boring technical reports, but Sara assured me that she would not let that happen to "our" book. It has been a joy to work with her. I have also enjoyed working with the production staff at Temple University Press: Kate Nichols, Joan Vidal, and David Wilson. While most of the original graphics and photographs were prepared by Rob Schultz while he was at the Commonwealth Heritage Group, the final plates were done by Kate Nichols and her staff, and the final maps were drawn by Nat Case. I wanted this book to be mainly pictures, and Kate Nichols as well as Rob have made that a reality. Many thanks. Jamie Armstrong completed a careful copyedit of the manuscript, which we all appreciate.

I am also grateful to Laura Stroffolino, curator of the Print and Picture Collection, Free Library of Philadelphia, for chasing down images for the book and putting up with my confusion about permissions. Randy Goss, photo archivist for the Delaware Public Archives, provided the image of the Lippincott Button Factory, and Jessica Rahmer, image rights manager at the St. Louis Art Museum, provided a digital copy of the beautiful painting of an eighteenth-century tavern. Last but not least thanks to Tyler Love, archivist and library manager for Independence National Historical Park, for finding a good image of the old visitor center, which the Museum of the American Revolution replaced.

I have been doing archaeology in Philadelphia for twenty years and have developed colleagues who feel like family. As usual, I turned to them during this project—Coxey Toogood for historical leads, Juliette Gerhardt for artifact explanations, Tod Benedict for documentary specifics, Sarah Ruch for graphic advice, and Wade Catts for corporate memory. Missed is Dan Roberts, who hired me to do urban archaeology before I knew how and would have totally approved of this project because he was dedicated to disseminating archaeological results to the general public. My personal friends have put up with this project as they have put up with many others. I am grateful for their tolerance of my workaholic tendencies and thank goodness that Andrea and Frank kept me walking and Ruth kept me reading.

Support for this publication was provided by the Museum of the American Revolution. It has been exciting to be part of the creation of Philadelphia's newest museum, and I am grateful for the museum's support and for the museum's president and CEO Michael Quinn's interest in archaeology.

ARCHAEOLOGY AT THE SITE OF
THE MUSEUM OF THE AMERICAN REVOLUTION

1

URBAN ARCHAEOLOGY
AND THE MUSEUM OF THE AMERICAN
REVOLUTION SITE

THE LAND AT THE CORNER of Chestnut and Third Streets in Philadelphia where the Museum of the American Revolution now stands was the site of an archaeological excavation during the summer of 2014. Anyone looking over the construction fence probably would not have been able to tell the archaeologists from the construction workers, but we were there. We worked side by side with the contractor, all of us in hard hats and work boots, with them and their big machines and us with our shovels and trowels (fig. 1.1).

Cities are complicated places, both aboveground and below. As they grow, they leave a complex muddle of foundations and fill buried beneath the present streetscape. The fill sometimes consists of rubble (from buildings that once stood on the site) mixed with soil, and sometimes it is just clean soil used to cover what was there before and to create a new building surface. This intertwined record of episodes of construction and destruction is often further complicated by crisscrossing utility trenches, which cut through the rubble of

Figure 1.1. Construction on the Museum of the American Revolution site at the southeast corner of Chestnut Street and Third Street, summer 2014. (Photograph by Tim Mancl.)

former structures and once open spaces. The Museum of the American Revolution Museum site was no different (fig. 1.2). The site covers one-quarter of a city block in the heart of the oldest part of Philadelphia. It had been developed and redeveloped many times since William Penn conceived of Philadelphia as a "green country town" in the 1680s. First it was a place to live and set up small shops and businesses. As the eighteenth century turned into the nineteenth, the site became more commercial, and by the end of the century the original small lots had been combined into larger ones to accommodate multistory buildings with deep basements. Similar buildings are still standing across from the museum on Chestnut

Figure 1.2. (*following spread*) Modern map showing the Museum of the American Revolution site in relation to Independence National Historical Park.

Street. The buildings on the site, however, were taken down during the creation of Independence National Historical Park in the 1950s. The National Park Service built its visitor center for Independence National Historical Park on the site in anticipation of the country's bicentennial, and it was that building that was demolished to make room for the Museum of the American Revolution (fig. 1.3).

An archaeological excavation was required on the museum site because the land originally belonged to the National Park Service. When the museum acquired the land, it came with the condition that an archaeological investigation be conducted. The National Historic Preservation Act (NHPA),

Figure 1.3. The visitor center built by the National Park Service in the 1970s in anticipation of the Bicentennial. Most of the building was demolished in the spring of 2014 to make room for the Museum of the American Revolution. (Courtesy of Independence National Historical Park.)

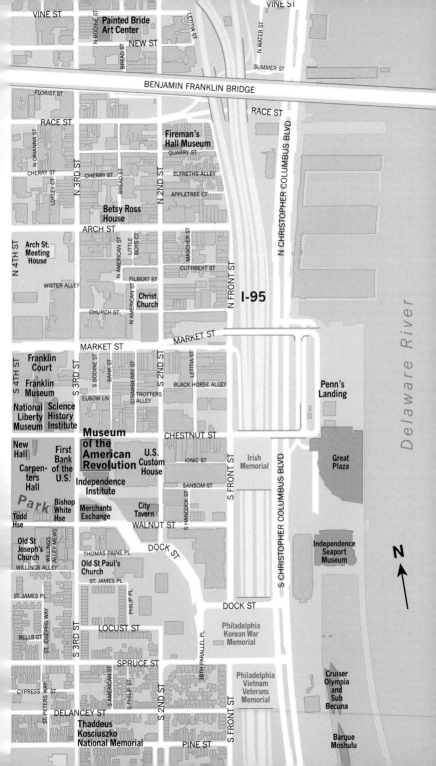

first passed in 1966, requires an archaeological study if a proposed construction project is on federal property or is built with federal funds. NHPA specifies a three-step process for evaluating a site and mitigating any damage to significant remains from the past that might be destroyed by the pending construction. The Park Service had already begun the process when the land was transferred to the museum.

STEP ONE—THE HISTORICAL STUDY OF THE SITE

In 2010 the National Park Service hired John Milner Associates, Inc. (now Commonwealth Heritage Group, Inc.) to do what is technically called an archaeological sensitivity study of the proposed museum site. This is the first stage of any study done under NHPA regulations. As the law requires, the sensitivity study traced the entire history of the site including the possibility of Native American occupation before the arrival of William Penn in 1682. The earliest map that shows the site area was drawn by surveyor Thomas Holme in 1683 (fig. 1.4). Made for William Penn, the map laid out two clusters of blocks, one beginning at the Delaware River and another beginning at the Schuylkill River. Both Holme and Penn envisioned the city growing inward from both rivers, but it did not happen that way. Subdivided into lots, the Delaware River blocks were developed first, and the museum site was among them.

Penn initially granted the site area to four individuals: Cornelius Boom, Henry Wood, John King, and William Carter. According to historical sources, William Hudson, a tanner and

Figure 1.4. *(facing page, side-turned)* Thomas Holme's plan for the City of Philadelphia, 1683. Its original title was *A Portraiture of the City of Philadelphia in the Province of Pennsylvania in America.*

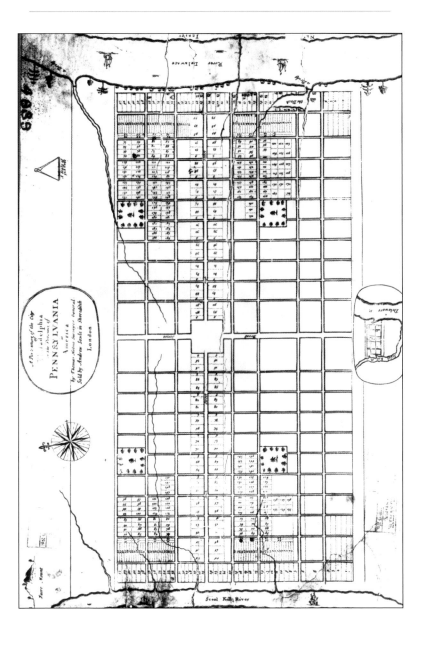

eventual mayor of Philadelphia, bought the lot at the corner of Third and Chestnut Streets (Boom's lot) before the end of the seventeenth century. There was already a house on the property, which may or may not have been the one described as Hudson's "mansion" by Thomas Glenn in a book published in 1891. The mansion was supposedly built of "red and black glazed brick," was three stories high, had a sloping roof, and was surrounded by a paved courtyard enclosed by a high wall. There were coach-way entrances on both Third and Chestnut Streets, stables and servant quarters at the rear of the courtyard, and a garden with "a charming view of the Delaware" that sloped down to Dock Creek. Dock Creek was the cove and branching stream that reached from the Delaware up to Third Street (fig. 1.5). Glenn's description of Hudson's house probably refers to later years, but the site where the museum stands was definitely occupied by the turn of the eighteenth century.[1]

By the end of the eighteenth century, the site included twenty-three historic lots (fig. 1.6). The lots were narrow, those on Chestnut Street generally measuring no more than 50 feet from east to west. They originally extended all the way to Dock Creek, a distance of more than 200 feet, but by the middle of the eighteenth century an alley (labeled Carter Street on fig. 1.6) running east and west subdivided the block. The lots facing Chestnut Street generally ran about 120 feet back to the alley, while the lots south of the alley were even smaller. The residents represented a mixture of artisans, probably keeping their shops on the ground floor and living with their families above. They included watchmakers, tailors, grocers, curriers

---

1. Information on the early development of the museum site is from Yamin et al. 2010. See also Yamin 2016. For further description of Hudson's house, see Glenn 1891.

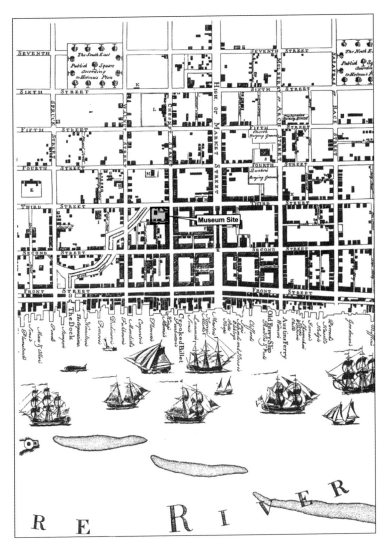

Figure 1.5. Detail of Scull map of Philadelphia, 1762, showing "the Dock" and the creek that reached up to Third Street just south of the Museum of the American Revolution site.

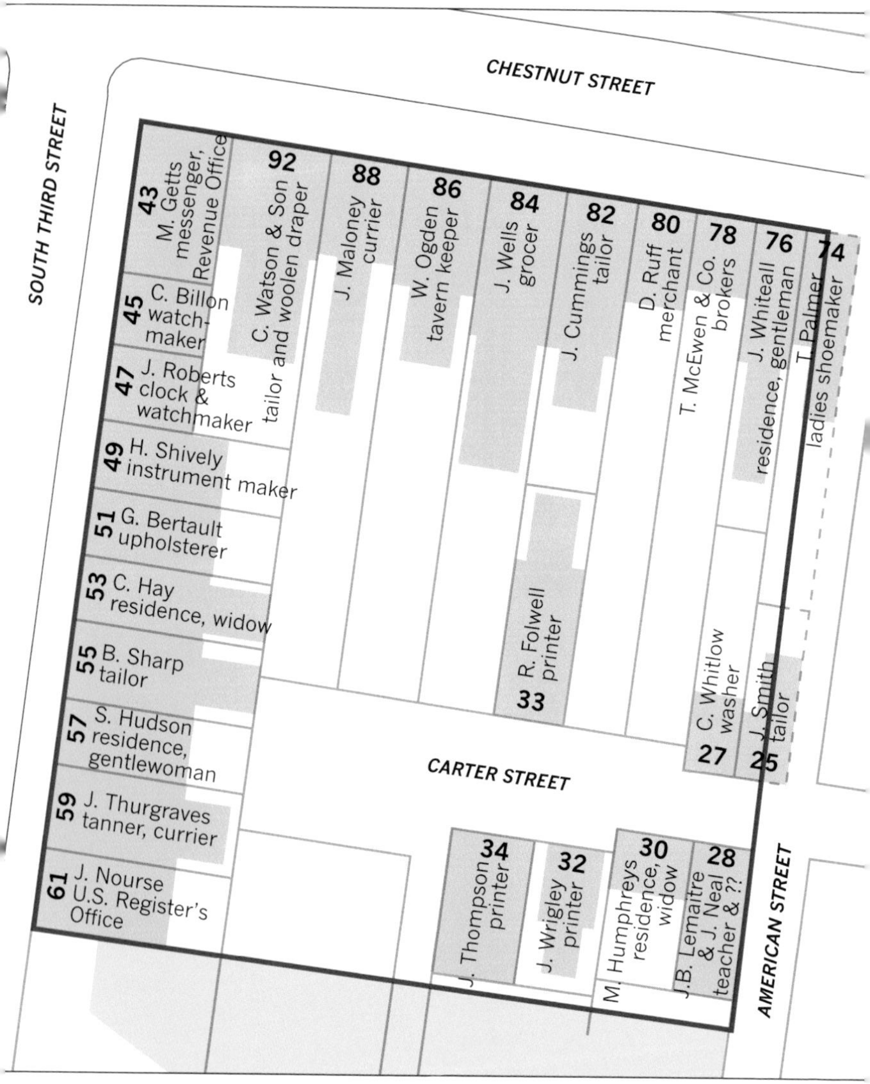

Figure 1.6. Map of historic lots and occupants on the Museum of the American Revolution site, ca. 1800. Based on a reconstruction from the 1799 direct tax and an 1800 city directory done by the National Park Service, 2009. (Independence National Historical Park Library.)

(leather processers), and printers, as well as a gentlewoman relative of William Hudson on Third Street and several widows. There was at least one merchant, a tavern keeper, a revenue office, and the brokers T. McEwen & Co. A historic rendering of a portion of the museum site shows how some of the structures along the south side of Chestnut Street looked at the end of the eighteenth century (fig. 1.7).

Neither rich nor poor eighteenth-century residents had indoor plumbing. They depended on privies, which they called "necessaries," in their backyards, and it is from those "necessaries" (as well as wells and cisterns) that urban archaeologists get their data. In Philadelphia, the privy shafts—that is, the

Figure 1.7. Historic drawing of dwellings on the south side of Chestnut Street, ca, 1800 (Courtesy of the Free Library of Philadelphia, Print and Picture Collection.)

Figure 1.8. Privy (feature 50) as it appeared from the top before bisecting for excavation.

holes dug beneath outhouses to contain human waste—were lined with brick (fig. 1.8). The generally circular shafts measured between four and five feet in diameter and may originally have been as much as twenty feet deep. The bricks were dry laid to allow liquid waste to seep through the walls into the ground, but solid wastes accumulated in the shafts. Citizen complaints about contamination of wells in the middle of the eighteenth century led to the passage of laws that restricted the depth of the privy shafts depending on where they were located in the city. As specified in the 1763 Act to Prevent and Remove Certain Nuisances in and near the City of Philadelphia, privies next to the Delaware River could only be six feet deep, while between Second and Third Streets (including the Museum of the American Revolution site) they could be fifteen feet deep. Archaeologists rarely find complete privy shafts in urban places since they tend to be truncated (have their tops cut off) by construction in areas that were once backyards. The very bottoms of the shafts, however, often survive later construction because they are so deeply buried in the ground. What remains at the bottoms of the privy shafts is what archaeologists get to excavate.[2]

Although privies were periodically cleaned, especially after citizens became sensitive to contamination, the accumulated waste—what we call night soil—at the bottom of the shafts often remained undisturbed. Night soil is characteristically dense, organic, and sticky. As you would expect, it has an unpleasant odor, although it is not the same as the odor of recent human waste. The density and texture of night soil tends to adhere to artifacts that are buried in it, often making them largely invisible. We screen all excavated soil through quarter-inch wire mesh to ensure the recovery of even the tiniest artifacts, but when screening night soil, we use water from a pressurized hose to get the soil through the screen. A big glob of night soil may at first look as if it contains nothing, but after it is sprayed with water the artifacts appear (fig. 1.9).

Night soil may also contain microscopic remains that provide information on diet and health. Before it is water screened, samples are taken for later analysis by ethnobotanists and parasitologists. Ethnobotanists identify seeds from

---

2. Tod Benedict (2004) conducted a study of all the shaft features including privies, cisterns, and wells that had been excavated archaeologically in Philadelphia between the 1950s and 2004. Much of the data presented here is drawn from Benedict's study, which summarizes all relevant structural data relating to the shafts and discusses the bricklayers, well diggers, hod carriers, privy cleaners, and carters involved in their construction and maintenance.

Figure 1.9. John Milner Associates (Commonwealth Heritage Group) crew screening excavated soil with the help of a hose.

food remains and medicinal plants that survive in the soil to learn more about what was eaten and used in the households responsible for the privy. Food remains, both plants and animals, provide archaeologists with information on the ethnicity and economic status of the people who deposited them. The identification of medicinal plants suggests which species were locally available as well as what physical ailments were treated. A parasitologist can identify the remains of parasites—different kind of worms, for instance—that may have been causing discomfort to members of the household.

What is particularly valuable about night soil deposits is that they relate to people who were living on a particular historic property at a particular time. The artifacts buried in the night soil and even seeds and other food remains can be connected to people whose names we can sometimes find in the documentary record. These people threw unwanted possessions in their privies because they had no other place to put them. Urban lots were small and there was no city garbage collection. Fill deposits—that is, soil mixed with artifacts or clean soil—in the upper portions of abandoned privies often date to a change in residence on a property, when one family moved out and another moved in, but night soil deposits found at the bottoms of privy shafts, dated by their artifact content, relate to peoples' everyday lives.

While the construction workers shored the edges of the excavation area on the Museum of the American Revolution site, we stood right next to them to watch for those shafts and anything else that might relate to eighteenth- and nineteenth-century occupation of the site (fig. 1.10). Field director Tim Mancl sometimes observed the construction activities

Figure 1.10. Tod Benedict monitoring D'Angelo Brothers contractors as they remove overlying fill on the Museum of the American Revolution site, 2014. (Photograph by Tim Mancl.)

alone, but at other times archaeologists Tod Benedict and Kathryn Wood helped to clear dirt from a suspected shaft feature or make drawings and photographs of what was uncovered. Kevin Bradley, Meagan Ratini, Katherine McCormick, T. Patrick Snyder, and Alexandra Vanko joined the team once full archaeological excavation was underway.

STEPS TWO AND THREE— THE ARCHAEOLOGICAL INVESTIGATION

Urban archaeology is a messy affair. The challenge is to find the shafts (privies, wells, or cisterns) buried beneath layers and layers of structural remains and fill. Once shafts and other structural features such as historic foundations are identified, the next step is to determine their potential to produce significant information about the past. For those that show promise, the third step is to excavate, record, and analyze the remains. Determinations of potential significance are made by the principal investigator, who in this case worked with Jed Levin, who oversaw the excavation for the National Park Service, which had required the excavation in the first place.

To begin the process of finding buried structures, we need the help of skilled construction workers, especially machine operators, to carefully scrape off the deep fill that covers anything that might be significant archaeologically. The fill is removed under an archaeologist's supervision. If we see something—an old foundation or a circle of brick that might be a privy or well, for instance—we ask the machine operator to stop digging so we can take a look. Sometimes the "something" requires hand excavation and sometimes it requires only a written description, photograph, or drawing. Whichever it is, the archaeologists and the contractor work together to complete what needs to be done as efficiently as possible. This is not easy for anyone. It slows down the contractor's work, and it puts the archaeologists under pressure to record information from the past in less than ideal circumstances. Good communication is essential, and the more both the contractor and the archaeologists know about each other's responsibilities the more likely it is that the project will go smoothly.

MUSEUM SITE SPECIFICS

The small-scale buildings that dominated the museum site during the first half of the nineteenth century were replaced with multistoried commercial buildings in the second half of the century (fig. 1.11). Besides displacing old buildings,

Figure 1.11. Historic panorama of Chestnut Street east of Third Street, Philadelphia, 1857, attributed to Schnabel, Finkeldey, Demme. (Courtesy of the Free Library of Philadelphia, Print and Picture Collection.)

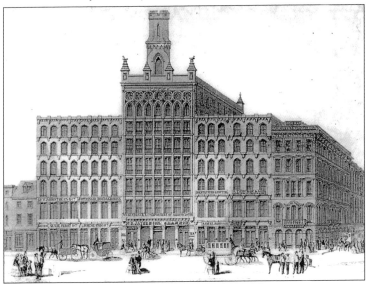

Figure 1.12. Photograph of the parking lot on the site of the Museum of the American Revolution after the nineteenth-century buildings on the site had been taken down by the National Park Service in the 1950s. (Independence National Historical Park Library.)

the new buildings covered over the open spaces that were originally the backyards and alleyways typical of the eighteenth-century urban landscape. Some of the commercial buildings on the museum site had two basements, one on top of the other, reaching depths of about seventeen feet, making it likely that if any shafts were found they would be under the basement floors. When the National Park Service took the commercial buildings down in the 1950s they did not remove the basements. Instead they filled the basements with building rubble and covered the rubble with many feet of fill. A parking lot was built on top of the fill in the 1950s (fig. 1.12), and the visitor center took its place in 1976. The visitor center did not have a basement, which meant that the earlier nineteenth-century basements were likely still intact below the building. That also meant that if shaft features were sealed beneath basement floors when the buildings were first taken down, the features would still be there.

Dismantling the visitor center was not as easy as anticipated. Removing the bell tower, in particular, took more time and more brute force than the contractor had expected. An archaeologist was on site during this process just in case anything archaeological turned up. Nothing did, and we got ready for the real thing. Work began on July 28, 2014.

Even though we had maps showing how the site looked before it was cleared in the 1950s, we wanted to know the exact layout so we could match the historic lots with the people who lived on them. Finding Carter's Alley seemed the best way to know where we were on the ground. As the contractor began to dig beneath where the visitor center had been, we looked for remnants of the alley (called Carter Street on fig. 1.6). Carter's Alley marked the backs of the Chestnut Street properties, and once we found it we could locate the properties on either side of it. Carter's Alley had been open until the Park Service built the visitor center in the 1970s.

There was also the possibility that the ground surface below the alley had never been disturbed and might seal remnants of Native American activities. Tim Mancl, who directed the archaeological excavation on a day-to-day basis, carefully guided the backhoe operator to scrape off layers of dirt where maps indicated the alley should have been. First to appear were two brick-lined drains that seemed to mark the northern edge of the alley. A foundation marked the southern edge, and another wall crosscut the alley from north to south (fig. 1.13). A small brick circle in the center of the alley appeared

EXCAVATING THE WELL

Tim Mancl, the field director, took on the task of excavating the well found in Carter's Alley. The well measured just 2.8 feet across, but it went down fourteen feet, a long way to excavate by hand. It was mainly filled with silty sand mixed with clinkers, gravel, and brick fragments. To stay in compliance with OSHA (the federal agency that sets workplace safety standards) regulations, which don't allow work in a confined space more than five feet deep, Tim dismantled the brick shaft as he went down. Water began to seep in at about eight feet, and much of the excavation was done in high rubber boots.

As the profile drawing shows, the top 6.5 feet of the well's brick walls rested on a wooden ring below which the exterior of the brick was sheathed in vertical wooden planks. The planks were probably put in place to create a form for the bricks which were laid inside them. The top of the pump shaft appeared just above the wooden ring and continued to just below another wooden ring at the base of the well walls. The wooden pump shaft was made in two parts. A tapered upper section fit into an octagonal iron ring that connected

Facing page: **Tim Mancl excavating the well found in Carter's Alley.**

Above: **The bottom of the well shaft once excavation was complete.**

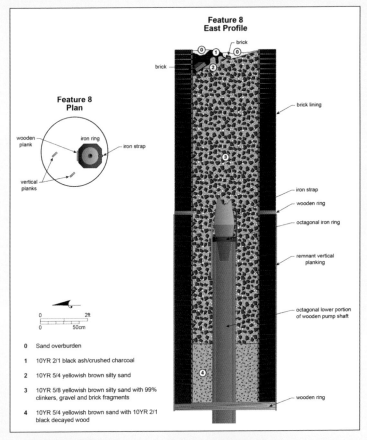

Feature 8
East Profile

brick

brick

brick lining

iron strap

wooden ring

octagonal iron ring

remnant vertical planking

octagonal lower portion of wooden pump shaft

wooden ring

Feature 8
Plan

wooden plank

iron ring

iron strap

vertical planks

0   2ft
0   50cm

0   Sand overburden

1   10YR 2/1 black ash/crushed charcoal

2   10YR 5/4 yellowish brown silty sand

3   10YR 5/8 yellowish brown silty sand with 99% clinkers, gravel and brick fragments

4   10YR 5/4 yellowish brown sand with 10YR 2/1 black decayed wood

Profile of the well shaft drawn by Tim Mancl and Robert Schultz.

with an iron strap and thin wooden plank to the lower portion of the shaft. Most of the upper section had rotted away, but it originally would have led to the aboveground pumping mechanism. The lower portion of the pump shaft was largely intact. It extended down about six feet below the octagonal iron ring and had a water intake hole just above the wooden ring at the bottom.

The well predated the construction of Dr. Jayne's proto-skyscraper (see Chapter 5) but was probably in use during his time and closed after the fire that seriously damaged his building in 1872. At least one Dr. Jayne expectorant bottle was found in the thin layer of ash and charcoal at the top of the shaft.■

Figure 1.13. Archaeologists recording Carter's Alley after it was uncovered. From left to right: Megan Ratini, Kevin Bradley (with dustpan), Kathryn Wood (on bucket), Alexandra Vanko, and T. Patrick Snyder. (Photograph by Tim Mancl, 2014.)

to be a well, just the kind of truncated shaft we hoped to find (see sidebar).

Carter's Alley proved to be an anchor for the rest of the excavation. There was no evidence of Native American occupation, but shaft features were found south of the alley and north of it (fig. 1.14). Other kinds of features—fifty-two in all—were also found, including foundation fragments, floors from different periods, and even a cast-iron door that had led to a tunnel under the alley. Not all the features could be connected to former site residents, but those that could tell a story of the Museum of the American Revolution site from its beginnings

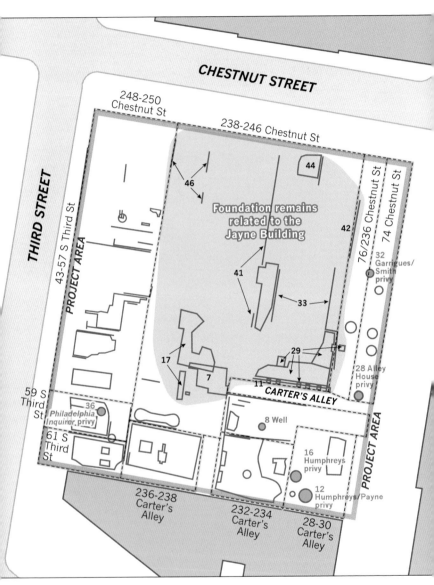

Figure 1.14. Site plan showing the archaeological features uncovered by John Milner Associates archaeologists on the Museum of the American Revolution site, 2014.

at the end of the seventeenth century to the Second World War more than two hundred years later. Such a long material record of change is unusual in an urban context. It amounts to a veritable archaeological history of Philadelphia in microcosm. Eighteenth- and nineteenth-century features have been excavated on other sites in Philadelphia, but only rarely has archaeology revealed the evolution of a site from the very earliest days of the city to the middle of the twentieth century.

While we did not know what specific artifacts we would find in the shafts, we could tell from their intact outlines that they were undisturbed enough to contain artifacts deposited in the eighteenth and nineteenth centuries. The next step was to excavate those shafts layer by layer and recover the artifacts.

2

EARLY RESIDENTS AND WHAT
THEY LEFT BEHIND

THE EARLIEST EVIDENCE for eighteenth-century life on the Museum of the American Revolution site came from two privies, one that probably belonged to a very small house that faced an alley marking the eastern boundary of the site and one on the properties that faced Chestnut Street at its eastern end (features 28 and 32 on fig. 1.14). The archaeological evidence from the house on the alley dated to the very beginning of the eighteenth century. It suggests that people were living on the alley as early as they were living on Chestnut Street. The alley's name changed over the years: it was called Smith's Alley in the middle of the eighteenth century, and in the later eighteenth century its southern section was called Goforth's Alley. It became Exchange Street and later Exchange Place in the nineteenth century before finally becoming American Street. We do not know the names of all the people who lived on the alley and on Chestnut Street in the early years, but most of those we do seem to have been associated with the tanning industry in one way or another.

The tanning industry and the problems it created seem to have been characteristic of many early American cities.[1] Although very little is known about the industry specifically in Philadelphia, tanning required conditions that were present in the vicinity of Dock Creek. The tanning process begins with the washing and scraping of animal hides followed by dunking them in pits of lime water to dissolve any remaining hair. Once thoroughly washed and softened the hides are put in vats filled with a chemical tanning solution made of tannin derived from oak bark. These initial steps required standing water, which was available in the swampy area around Dock Creek. After the hides are soaked, the running water of the creek was used to wash away the chemicals and rinse the hides. Laborers used long handled hooks to move the skins around in the various solutions and finally to remove them for drying. In Philadelphia, as elsewhere, the process fouled the environment creating what were called nuisance conditions characterized by putrefying carcasses, contaminating wastes, and terrible smells.

LIFE ON THE ALLEY

Four brick shafts were uncovered along the eastern edge of the Museum of the American Revolution site. Although three of the shafts had been mostly filled with concrete, the one at the south end of the line, labeled feature 28 on figure 1.14, contained an assemblage of artifacts that dated to the early years of the eighteenth century. The artifacts were found below a thick layer of soil that included many cattle horns (fig. 2.1).

---

1. For a description of an excavation that identified eighteenth-century tanning in New York City, see Yamin and Schuldenrein 2007.

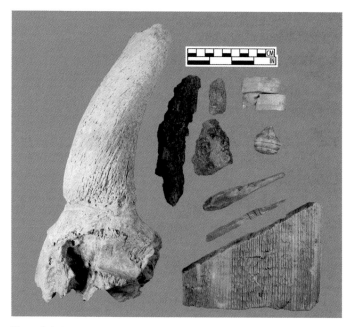

Figure 2.1. Horn core, bark, wood shavings, modified wood, and cut plank found in the upper fill of the alley house privy (feature 28). (Photograph by Juliette Gerhardt.)

The horns appeared to be debris from a tanyard located on Dock Creek just down the hill from the site.

As early as 1739 Benjamin Franklin and others recognized the threat of environmental degradation to peoples' health and petitioned the city's assembly to have the tanneries removed. The wealthy tanyard owners, however, defended their right to "exist in the center of town and to use Dock Creek as an open conduit for their wastes." Although public sentiment and even the assembly favored Franklin's proposals for cleaning up the Dock by laying out sewers and building docking facilities for small boats, it never happened. Finally, in the 1760s the creek was channeled and covered over.

We cannot know who deposited the horn cores in the privy on the museum site, but it is likely that the waste, which in addition to horn cores included leather scraps and bark fragments, was part of the early cleanup effort. The artifacts recovered from the privy date to the 1720s and 1730s, the very period when problems with Dock Creek were first recognized. The lot where the privy was found was owned by William Carter, but it was occupied by a tanner named William Pyewell. The privy may have belonged to Pyewell or to someone who rented a small house that faced the six-foot-wide alley that ran along the eastern edge of the property down to Dock Creek. Although the alley did not have a name in Carter's day, the next owner of the property, William Smith, gave it his name. It is actually from Smith's administration, a document similar to a will, that we know about the "alley house," which at Smith's death in 1764 was rented to Hannah Howell. We do not know the names of the people who rented the alley house in the 1730s, but findings suggest they may have come from Germany.

Two very distinctive artifacts found in the privy were manufactured in Germany. One was an almost complete Westerwald stoneware jug with blue cobalt decoration, and the other was the base of a more unusual Westerwald jug with Knibis (fanlike) decoration (fig. 2.2). Westerwald is a mountainous region on the bank of the Rhine River in western Germany. With their distinctive blue cobalt decoration and geometric designs, Westerwald jugs were exported to America through England in the early eighteenth century and appear in archaeological contexts up to the Revolutionary War (Noel-Hume 1969: 276–285). Germans were one of the first large immigrant groups in Philadelphia. According to one scholar, German emigration to Pennsylvania began as early as the

Figure 2.2. Jugs from the Westerwald region of Germany found at the bottom of the alley house privy (feature 28). (Photograph by Juliette Gerhardt.)

1690s and by the end of the 1720s was a virtual "human flood" (Bronner 1982: 37). In addition to the jugs, a variety of drinking paraphernalia were found in the privy, and it is easy to imagine a tired tanyard worker slogging up the hill from Dock Creek at the end of a long day—soaking wet from pushing hides around in the tanning vats—and finding comfort in a drink poured from a jug made in his homeland.

The number of fruit pits recovered from the privy—fourteen hundred, the majority of them from cherries—suggests that someone in the household was cooking with cherries. Perhaps the woman of the house baked pies to sell or put up cherry preserves, made brandied cherries, cherry bounce, or cherry wine. The four pie dishes, five butter pots, and three

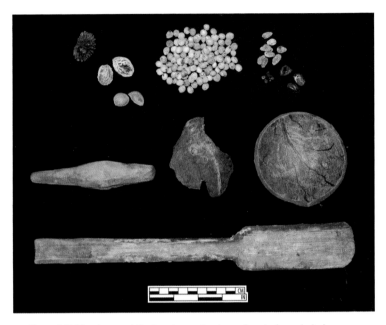

Figure 2.3. Wooden peel (bottom), wooden bung for closing a hole in a barrel, coconut shells (middle), cherry pits, and peach pits from the alley house privy (feature 28). (Photograph by Juliette Gerhardt.)

milk pans recovered from the upper fill in the privy would have been used in the kitchen. Of particular interest was the long-handled wooden artifact first identified as a spatula (fig. 2.3). The length of its handle and its flatness, however, suggest it was a peel, an implement used to take hot baked goods out of the oven.[2]

That everyone in the household was making money was typical of the period. Philadelphia's early immigrant residents were not rich; they needed to make a living, and they took

---

2. This interpretation was suggested by a visitor to the Museum of the American Revolution in June 2017 and supplemented by archaeologist Julia Costello.

to it with energy and ingenuity (Wood 1991: 325). Evidence suggests that, besides working in a tanyard and offering baked goods for sale, a member of the household may have worked in the nearby Anthony Duché pottery. Two gray stoneware tankards, a galley pot, a redware galley pot, and two glazed stoneware disks that appeared to be reworked saggers (pieces of pottery shaped to hold vessels in place while they are being fired) could have been brought home from the pottery on Chestnut Street, just one block away from the museum site.

LIFE ON CHESTNUT STREET

William Carter, the wealthy blockmaker who owned the property where the alley house was located, also owned a property on Second Street, where he likely lived. Blockmakers carved the wooden "blocks" or pulleys that were used to handle the rigging on ships. Carter also held a variety of political positions during his lifetime. William Penn appointed him an alderman for the city of Philadelphia in 1701; he was a judge for the city court, a member of the assembly, and served as Philadelphia's ninth mayor in 1711. At his death in 1738, Carter left his Chestnut Street property to a board of trustees with instructions to "grant and convey the property to such person or persons as the Philadelphia Monthly Meeting of Quakers should direct." Samuel Garrigues bought the western half of the property including a fifteen-foot three-inch frontage on Chestnut Street in 1744, and William Smith bought the eastern half with a fifteen-foot frontage on Chestnut Street in 1749. Both properties extended back to Carter's Alley, so named in honor of the original land owner. A privy found straddling the boundary between Garrigues's and Smith's lots was probably originally built by Carter, but the artifacts recovered from it date to Garrigues's and Smith's time (feature 32 on fig. 1.14). The challenge is determining which came from which household. But the historical record contains some clues.

Philadelphia Quaker Monthly Meeting records note that Samuel and Mary (née Ralph) Garrigues lived at 76 Chestnut Street with their ten children from at least 1744 to the mid-1760s. A redware charger, or platter, found at the bottom of the shared privy bears the date 1754, indicating that the deposit could not have been made any earlier. The charger may have celebrated the birth of Susannah Garrigues, who, according to Quaker meeting records, was born on July 31 of that year but died two years later. It is also possible that the date refers to when the charger was made as it resembles the style of Gottfried Aust, a potter who was working in Bethlehem, Pennsylvania, at the time. An advertisement published in the *Pennsylvania Journal* on February 2, 1764, described Garrigues as "living in Chestnut Street at the sign of the fifty-six-pound weight, nearly opposite the Three Tun Tavern . . . where all sorts of weights and measures were sold." "Sundry seals and weights" are listed in the inventory of goods attached to Garrigues's will (August 1783) and we also found weights in the privy (fig. 2.4). That does not mean that all the artifacts found in the privy came from the Garrigues household, but at least some of them did. The many marbles recovered probably belonged to the Garrigues children.

Besides selling weights and measures to shopkeepers Samuel Garrigues served as "Clerk of the Market," a job that required overseeing the daily activities of the market, which was located a block north of Chestnut Street in the middle of what was then known as High (now Market) Street (fig. 2.5). Like the residents of the alley house twenty or so years earlier, Garrigues worked hard to make a living. When he died in

Figure 2.4. Shells (top), lead weights (middle), and marbles (bottom) probably deposited by the Garrigues household in the shared privy (feature 32). (Photograph by Juliette Gerhardt.)

1783, his will referred to him as a "gentleman" and the inventory of goods attached to his will reflected a relatively well-off household worth £3,940.6.5. The privy on the museum site, however, was filled much earlier, probably when the next-door neighbor, William Smith, died in 1764 or soon after.

William Smith, a tanner who may have owned one of the tanneries on Dock Creek, bought the half of Carter's property next to the north–south alley that eventually bore his name. He was well connected, and in addition to his income from tanning, he controlled a considerable amount of property in the city, from which he collected rents. Among his rent-

Figure 2.5. The Market House where Samuel Garrigues was the clerk, a job that involved maintaining order in the market, assigning and inspecting stalls, weighing bread, checking scales, and inspecting fresh meat and other provisions. (After William Birch print.)

ers were Samuel Garrigues (next door), Joseph Ogden, the keeper of the Cross Keys Tavern at the northeast corner of Chestnut and Third Streets, Hannah Howell (tenant of the "alley house"), Isaac Morris, Samuel Hazell (storefront tenant), Richard Sewell, Captain Boon, Hugh Mean, Thomas Smith, Richard Tidmarsh, Mr. Erwin, William Watkins, and Robert Leavors. Smith's administration (a document performing the function of a will) listed £119.10.9 worth of household goods and innumerable expenses, some of which were incurred after his death. The household goods listed in the administration related mainly to eating and drinking. With the exception of a clock (worth £14.0.0) and clothing (worth £15.0.0), there were no high price items, and why the inventory included no furniture is a mystery. Perhaps his four grown sons and their wives incorporated all of their father's furniture into their own households. As for the rest of their father's possessions, they may have been thrown into the privy. Among the most personal items were wig curlers, fan parts, beads, buttons, and buckles (figs. 2.6 and 2.7). There were also lots of straight pins and many dishes. Straight pins were used in the eighteenth century as we use paper clips today. They held documents together, and it would not be surprising if William Smith needed many considering all the bookkeeping that managing of his properties must have required. The dishes, however, are difficult to assign to either household.

Figure 2.6. Wig curlers, beads, and fan parts probably from William Smith's household. (Photograph by Juliette Gerhardt.)

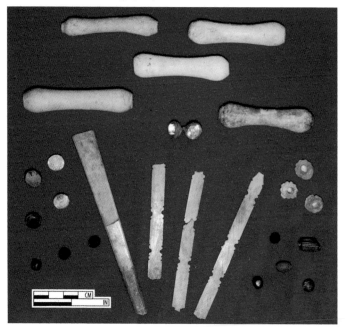

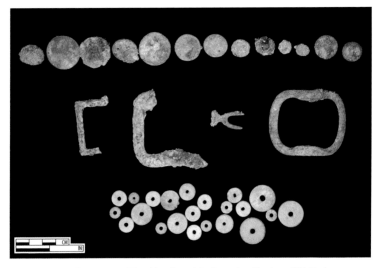

Figure 2.7. Buttons and buckles found in the privy (feature 32) that straddled the boundary between the Garrigues and Smith properties. (Photograph by Juliette Gerhardt.)

There were two sets of tin-glazed earthenware plates, one plain and one with beautiful hand-painted designs (fig. 2.8) plus a large (fifty-eight-piece) tea set made of Chinese export porcelain (fig. 2.9). The tea set, which would have been relatively expensive, included tea bowls, a coffee can, saucers, eleven slop bowls, and a creamer. While they might have belonged to the young Garrigues household, it is more likely that they were Mr. Smith's and were thrown out at his death. Both households were Quakers although the Philadelphia Monthly Meeting members list in 1772 noted that "Samuel Garrigues does not profess to be fully convinced of Friends principles, nor a desire to be considered as a Member in Unity, tho' he sometimes attends our religious Meetings." Quakers in Philadelphia did not necessarily keep to the "plain" style typical of Quakers elsewhere, at least in their house furnishings, so this elegant tea set would not have been unusual for a well-to-do Quaker home. Elizabeth Drinker, the wife of a wealthy Quaker merchant, kept a journal of her daily activities beginning in 1759, when she was in her twenties, until her death in 1807 (Goetz 1995). Nothing in the journal shows disdain for an elaborate style of life. The Drinkers had numerous servants and valuable furniture, which was seized in 1779 for Continental taxes. (To avoid supporting the war, some Quakers did not pay taxes.) The plain Quaker life seems to have been characterized by frequent attendance at meetings and disapproval of marriage by a priest—a reference to marrying a non-Quaker—, buying or selling Negroes, and excessive use of spirituous liquors.[3] There were some liquor bottles (one for gin and five for wine) in the shared privy, and also a few stemmed wine glasses and glass tumblers, but this privy contained many vessels that did not come from either Samuel Garrigues's household or William Smith's.

We believe that when the privy was closed, probably in anticipation of selling the property, some of the artifacts and dirt used to fill it came from the Three Tun Tavern across the street. In 1764, the *Pennsylvania Journal* described the Three Tun Tavern as "nearly opposite" Samuel Garrigues's weights and measures shop, and a 1768 *Pennsylvania Chronicle* advertisement "to let" the Three Tun Tavern reads, "The Olde Three Tun Tavern now the Fountain Inn in Chestnut Street lately accommodated with a new room back, forty feet long, very convenient for the entertainment of any public associa-

---

3. Gleaned from the author's review of Philadelphia Yearly Meeting minutes of 1753–1756, 1773, 1776, and 1781 at the Friends Historical Library, Swarthmore College, Swarthmore, PA.

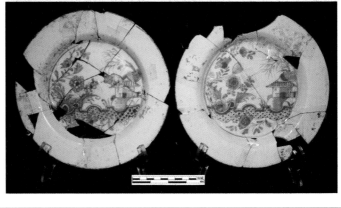

Figure 2.9. Chinese export porcelain teaware from the privy (Feature 32) that straddled the Garrigues and Smith properties. (Photograph by Juliette Gerhardt.)

tion and fellowship, together with a large stable, hay loft, etc. . . . For terms apply to Joseph Yeates, living on the premises." Perhaps during the renovations, Yeates threw out the old tavern equipage and took advantage of the privy across the street to get rid of the goods. Anthony Fortune, the new manager, probably set a fancier table for the gentlemen clientele he aimed to attract.

It would not be unusual for a privy to be filled with material that did not necessarily come from the property where it was located. In fact, there has been a long running debate

Figure 2.8. *(facing page)* Hand-painted tin-glazed earthenware plates from the privy (feature 32) that straddled the boundary between the Garrigues and Smith properties. (Photograph by Juliette Gerhardt.)

in Philadelphia over the source of privy fills. After passage of the 1763 law limiting the depth of privies, people sometimes filled them with whatever they could get to mask depths that were no longer allowed. The permitted depth on the museum site was fifteen feet, and it is likely that the Garrigues/Smith privy was considerably deeper. Since Samuel Garrigues was clerk of the market, an official city job, he may have been particularly compliant with regulations. It is also possible that, in the process of cleaning up their father's property for sale, William Smith's sons welcomed fill for the privy from wherever they could get it. They did not sell his property until 1771 although they continued to pay their father's debts and taxes (e.g., watch and lamp tax, poor tax, county tax, province tax) after his death. They also made renovations to the house, presumably to keep it in a rentable or saleable condition. As listed in Smith's administration, Michael Fish was paid for plastering in 1766; the next year James Claypool was paid for mending windows, and in 1769 John Houck received £2.0.0 for eight days of painting, and Samuel Garrigues received £23.0.0 for "half of the wall he finding the bricks" and "lime for the same." The reference to lime suggests that Garrigues's repairs related to the shared privy. It is not inconceivable that William Smith's sons rented their father's house for some of the time between his death in 1764 and when it was sold, although rents collected for that address are not mentioned in the administration. The artifacts recovered, however, suggest that the privy was closed in the late 1760s, the same time the tavern across the street was renovated.

The artifacts recovered from privies tell us about peoples' possessions, and we do our best to figure out what the possessions meant to their owners. We unfortunately cannot look into the peoples' minds. We can only speculate. Artifacts associated with a public place, in this case a tavern, are different. They provide a window into public life and activities outside of families rather than inside them. The Three Tun Tavern was such a place.

3

ARGUING THE REVOLUTION—A CHESTNUT STREET TAVERN IN THE 1760S

THE BLOCK where the Museum of the American Revolution now stands had the most taverns of any block in colonial-period Philadelphia. Everyone drank (the average annual per capita consumption of hard liquor was 3.7 gallons), and men in particular drank in public as well as private places (Rorabaugh 1979). You had to have a license to sell liquor, and the demand for tavern licenses in eighteenth-century Philadelphia outstripped the supply. There is proof of more than 100 petitions for tavern licenses submitted between 1704 and 1760 in the archives of the Historical Society of Pennsylvania, some granted and some not. A criterion seemed to be whether the petitioner's motive was merely opportunistic. A request out of temporary economic desperation was less likely to win approval than one from a person who seemed to be serious about entering the business of selling alcohol.

Until the middle of the eighteenth century, most taverns were run out of the front room of someone's residence. Men generally sat around a single table drinking from pewter cans

Figure 3.1. Typical eighteenth-century tavern scene. *Sea Captains Carousing in Surinam, 1752–58* by John Greenwood, American, 1727–1792. (Courtesy of the St. Louis Art Museum.)

or a shared punch bowl that was passed from one person to the next (fig. 3.1). It is easy to see how this arrangement promoted camaraderie, a kind of "enforced intimacy" (Thompson 1999: 3). Scholars claim that men of all different ranks drank together in these early taverns. They discussed politics in "an atmosphere free from deference" that helped create a political culture in Philadelphia "uncommonly open to the influence of laboring men" (Thompson 1999: 19). It was not until a decade or so before the Revolutionary War that taverns began to cater to like-minded groups of people. Laboring men were no longer welcome among the political elite who drank with their own kind in places like the City Tavern, which opened in 1773. The Three Tun Tavern was probably the egalitarian kind until it was transformed into the Fountain Inn, which its

manager, Anthony Fortune, advertised in 1771 as "aimed at a gentlemanly clientele." The dishes dumped in the Garrigues/ Smith privy apparently did not fit its new image.

THE THREE TUN TAVERN

Tavern artifacts (bottles, punch bowls, and other drinking vessels) are distinctive. They reflect the drinking of alcoholic beverages, of course, and are often found alongside smoking pipes, which men probably clenched between their teeth as they argued the issues of the day. The tavern artifacts recovered from the Smith/Garrigues privy resemble artifacts recovered from colonial-period taverns elsewhere. There were forty-one posset cups and five vessels of buff earthenware

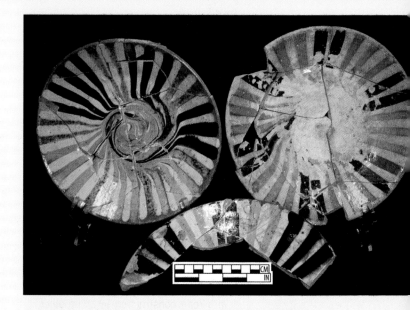

MADE IN PHILADELPHIA, REDWARE

While they may be decorated in a variety of ways, redwares, as suggested by their name, are made of common red clay. Philadelphia redwares are distinctive, but they are not all the same. Juliette Gerhardt, who analyzed the ceramics from the Museum of the American Revolution site, identified four different styles and was even able to identify the potters who made them. With one exception, they were made within three blocks of the museum site. The exception was a group of vessels made in Bethlehem, Pennsylvania, or possibly in Philadelphia in the Moravian tradition. The beautiful charger decorated with a pomegranate (fig. 3.5) is an example in the Moravian tradition. According to Gerhardt's research, Moravians interpreted pomegranates as a metaphor for Christ's blood and sacrifice.

Vessels made by the Hillegas brothers, who had a shop on Second Street in Philadelphia from the 1720s to 1746, used designs characteristic of slipwares made in the Low Countries. The Hillegas

Above and facing page: Bowls with unusual pinwheel designs, possibly made by Moravian master potter Gottfied Aust in 1754, or by one of his apprentices.

brothers were French Huguenots of German descent, and their products generally have folded and tooled rims as well as incised wavy lines on plain wares that resemble wares made in Holland.

The most unusual domestic redwares from the museum site were seven bowls decorated with a kind of pinwheel design that ends in a swirl in the centers of the bowls. The stripes that make up the pinwheels were sometimes black, green, and orange and sometimes just orange and green on a yellow ground. Gerhardt's research turned up two possible sources for these designs. They might have been made by Gottfried Aust in North Carolina. Aust, a member of the Moravian Church, emigrated from Herrnhut, Germany, in 1754 and spent ten months in Bethlehem, Pennsylvania, before going to North Carolina to join a Moravian community. It is possible that he introduced the pinwheel pattern to his brethren in Bethlehem, who may have shared it with their brethren in Philadelphia. Similar bowls were made by William Rogers, an English potter working in Virginia. An even more tantalizing possibility is that the pattern derived from France. A recent excavation associated with road construction in Montpellier, France, unearthed a kiln site that produced a large number of vessels in seventeenth-century contexts that were decorated with a virtually identical pattern to the one on the bowls from the museum site. It is clear that a variety of European traditions contributed to the style of redwares made in Philadelphia during the eighteenth century. ■

(Much of the information presented here is drawn from Gerhardt 2016.)

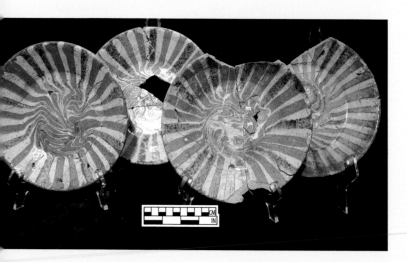

Figure 3.2. British-made, slip-decorated posset cups attributed to the Three Tun Tavern but found in the Garrigues-Smith privy. (Photograph by Juliette Gerhardt.)

with slipped line and dot decorations (fig. 3.2). Posset combined curdled milk with wine or ale, which sounds awful but was a popular warm drink in eighteenth-century Britain and America. There were also twenty-one tankards, some made in Britain (fig. 3.3) and some made in the colonies (fig. 3.4) in addition to fifteen punch bowls, clearly too many for a private household or even for the combination of two households. Punch was made from fruit juice spiked with rum, whiskey, or brandy. Customers drank various hard liquors—whiskey and rum were the most common—from the tankards and posset from the posset cups.

By the third quarter of the eighteenth century, food was being served in taverns, and the Three Tun Tavern may well have offered meals. The bones of edible mammals found in the privy, many with butchering marks, mainly came from large mutton roasts, an inexpensive cut that would have made good tavern fare. There were also dishes that were probably used to pass around accompaniments to the roasts. Local potters made the dishes out of local red clays. The largest, called

Figure 3.3. British-made tankards attributed to the Three Tun Tavern but found in the Garrigues-Smith privy. (Photograph by Juliette Gerhardt.)

Figure 3.4. American made tankards attributed to the Three Tun Tavern but found in the Garrigues-Smith privy. (Photograph by Juliette Gerhardt.)

Figure 3.5. Redware charger with pomegranate decoration found in the Garrigues-Smith privy but probably from the Three Tun Tavern. Attributed to the Moravian potters of Bethlehem, Pennsylvania. (Photograph by Juliette Gerhardt.)

chargers, were slip-decorated with various naturalistic motifs, and bowls of different sizes had swirled designs in many colors (fig. 3.5). These beautiful vessels would bring high prices in today's market but were very inexpensive when they were made. The Three Tun Tavern keeper served his customers on wares that would cost little to replace if broken.

The clay smoking pipes recovered are different. They belonged to customers, and the long stems, in particular, got broken all the time (fig. 3.6). A total of 180 pipe fragments were recovered from the privy. If pipes and ceramic vessels are added together, pipes make up 65 percent of the total. That is a good percentage, although it is not as high as the percentage found at other urban tavern sites. Ninety percent of the combined ceramic assemblage from the Lovelace Tavern in New York City, for instance, was made up of clay pipes. The pipes suggest that tavern clientele did not just stop by for a quick drink. They lingered to socialize, gossip, and learn the news. In some instances, they even stayed around for a dancing lesson or to learn a new language. In 1757, Jacob Ehrenzeller, the keeper of the Hand and Arm tavern on Arch Street in Philadelphia, "hosted an evening school where gentlemen might be taught German in the best fashion" (Thompson 1999: 82). But in mid-eighteenth-century Philadelphia, taverns were primarily places for talking, especially about politics.

Figure 3.6. Clay pipe bowls and stems similar to the 180 clay pipe fragments found in the Garrigues-Smith privy. The pipes shown came from a privy excavated on the site of the Independence Visitor Center on Independence Mall. (Photograph by Juliette Gerhardt.)

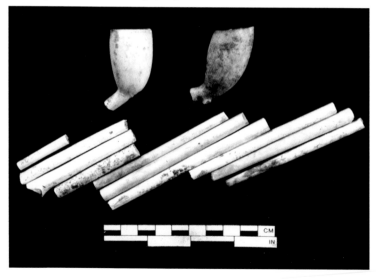

Political disputes raged in Philadelphia in the 1760s, and many debates surely took place in the Three Tun Tavern. Some issues had been argued from the very beginning of the colony: the position of Quakers vis a vis other groups, for instance, or whether a militia should be raised with indentured servants or not raised at all. One of the issues being argued in the period when the Three Tun Tavern became the Fountain Inn was whether Pennsylvania should remain a proprietary state or become a royal colony. Benjamin Franklin and Joseph Galloway were in favor of becoming a royal colony, and they promoted their position in Philadelphia's taverns by encouraging the already well-established custom of "treating," or buying drinks for tavern patrons. Treating was clearly intended to woo takers to one side of an argument or the other.[1] Although Philadelphia taverns at midcentury were places where the rich, the poor, and the middling sat side by side, showing neither disdain nor deference for the other, money was used to influence opinion. As arguments about this issue and others became more incendiary, some leaders, Benjamin Franklin among them, began "to doubt that drinkers in taverns expressed any opinion other than those planted artfully by incendiaries, demagogues, or a designing proprietary interest" (Thompson 1999: 143).

There was a movement to get electioneering out of the taverns and there was also a movement to establish more exclusive drinking venues for the elite. The conversion of the old Three Tun Tavern to the Fountain Inn was apparently part of that movement. Anthony Fortune, who owned the property, ran an ad in the *Pennsylvania Gazette* in 1771 that explicitly said his newly appointed inn was aimed at a gentlemanly cli-

1. This practice is discussed in detail in chapter 4 of Thompson 1999.

entele. The ad described the new inn's "long room" as suitable for the reception of juries or any set of "gentlemen" to the number of sixty or more on "private or public" business (quoted in Thompson 1999: 145). Joseph Yeates's tenure as tavern keeper and the dishes discarded in the Smith/Garrigues privy were remnants of an earlier time.

JOSEPH YEATES AND JAMES ORONOCO DEXTER

Joseph Yeates was granted a license to sell liquor in July 1763, at which time he likely came to the Three Tun Tavern. Tavern keepers generally rented the premises they oversaw and hired employees to help them do the work. One of the people who worked for Yeates in the 1760s was an enslaved man named James Oronoco Dexter. We know that because in 1767, a year before Yeates ran the ad "to let" the Three Tun Tavern, he contributed half the price of Dexter's manumission. The manumission paper (fig. 3.7) reads as follows:

> Know all men by these present that we the subscribers surviving Trustees for the Creditors of James Dexter and to whom the Estate of the said James Dexter both real and personal was in trust made over have received thro the Hands of Joseph Yeates and of Oronoko royal slave one hundred pounds full compensation for the said Oronoko and therefore neither we our heirs Exr. nor any of the Creditors of the said James Dexter do or can claim any Right in or to the said Oronoko. In witness whereof we have hereunto set our Hands and Seal this third Day.

It was signed and sealed in the presence of Asheton Humphreys, William Claire, Christopher Marshall, Charles

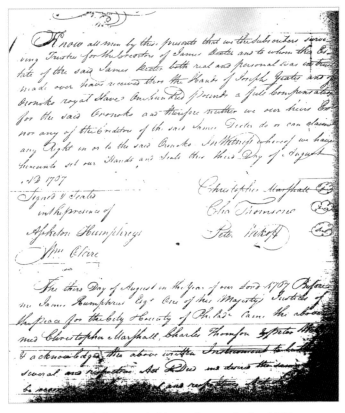

Figure 3.7. Manumission record of James Oronoco Dexter, 1768.

Thompson, and Peter Wikoff. Marshall, a retired pharmacist, had a chemical and paints shop just down the block. He is well known for keeping a diary in the years running up to the Revolutionary War when he was a delegate to the Philadelphia Provincial Council and twice appointed to the Continental Committee of Council and Safety. Dexter had apparently been hired out by his master to Yeates, and when his master, also named James Dexter, died, Oronoco became property of his creditors. From them he purchased his freedom, with fifty pounds that he earned himself and another fifty pounds contributed by Yeates. In the same year, Dexter purchased the freedom of Priss, who became his wife, for the sum of sixty pounds.

After leaving the employ of the Three Tun Tavern, Dexter worked as a coachman for John Pemberton, a wealthy Quaker merchant and traveling religious preacher. Dexter lived in the Pemberton household at least part of that time, but by 1790 he was living at 84 N. Fifth Street in a house he rented from Ebenezer Robinson, a brush maker who had apparently built the house as a rental property. Seven other people lived in Dexter's household including his second wife, Sarah. The house site was excavated in 2003 by the consulting company Kise Straw and Kolodner because it was in an area slated to become a bus parking lot for the Constitution Center, then under construction on the third block of Independence Mall.

The excavation of the Dexter residence turned up several backyard shaft features, only one of which could definitely be connected to the time when Dexter lived there. Ceramics recovered were primarily made of red-bodied earthenware and probably came from vessels used in the kitchen (e.g., milk pans and porringers), but there were a few fragments of Chinese porcelain teaware, several broken ceramic pieces, or sherds, from a green-glazed creamware plate, and a good number of clay pipe bowls (thirty-nine). As discussed above, pipes are often interpreted as a sign of active socializing.

As a free man, James Oronoco Dexter was a leading member of Philadelphia's African American community. He was one of six Philadelphia free blacks who petitioned the state of Pennsylvania in 1782 "to fence in the Negroes Burying Ground in the Potters field" (a portion of Wash-

The following short vignette weaves archaeological and historical data together to imagine what might have been on Joseph Yeates's mind. It is a technique I have used elsewhere to bring the past to life and make sense of what we have found (Yamin 1998).

WEAVING IT ALL TOGETHER, JOSEPH YEATES

It was not easy keeping a tavern on Chestnut Street in the 1760s. There was the occasional problem of an overly boisterous crowd of drinkers, but more serious was the problem of keeping help. Dexter (Yeates called him Noke) had been dependable, but the others kept disappearing. Now it was Thomas Currell, the new boy he had hired, nice enough but too young—just sixteen—to be on his own. Yeates advertised the runaway in the *Pennsylvania Gazette*:

> Runaway from the subscriber . . . a servant lad born in England . . . well set, full faced, fair complexion, and has brown hair. Had on, when he went away, a white broadcloth coat, with white metal buttons, old red jacket, linen trousers, and a blue surtout coat, with yellow metal buttons. He has been seen since he went away about the barracks, and other parts of town. Whoever secures said servant, so that his master may have him again, shall receive, if taken in town, twenty shillings and thirty if taken in the country with all reasonable charges paid.

He was worth much more to the no-longer-young Joseph Yeates though. What would he have done without Thomas when that runaway sorrel mare appeared in the tavern's stable in April of 1768? They couldn't afford to keep another horse and a pregnant one at that. It was Thomas who took care of her, and it was Thomas who carried all the broken tavernware across the street to help Mr. Smith's sons fill up the privy before they sold the property. He needed Thomas, and he missed Noke. He was glad he had contributed half of Noke's manumission—he couldn't deny him his freedom—but he needed help. The Three Tun was too much to handle alone.

Joseph Yeates died in 1770, just a year after Thomas Currell ran away. ∎

Information drawn from ads run in the *Pennsylvania Gazette* April 28, 1768, and Feb. 9, 1769, and a death notice in the *Pennsylvania Chronicle*, Nov. 26, 1770.

ington Square), and he was a founding member of St. Stephen's African Episcopal Church. Anna Coxe Toogood, a historian for Independence National Historical Park, thinks the organizational meeting for the church may have taken place in Dexter's house at 84 N. Fifth Street in 1794. Church records show that Dexter was one of several deacons or elders who guided the construction of the church. His particular responsibility appears to have been the procuring of stone for the foundation. By 1796 he was a vestryman, and a church ledger shows Dexter managing its financial affairs between 1795 and 1796. As indicated in the ledger, he and others advanced their own money for various tasks and were later reimbursed by the church. A single repayment of £270 from the church to Dexter suggests he had plenty of money to lend, and Doug Mooney, who directed the excavation on the Dexter house site and spent many hours at the historical society chasing down everything he could concerning Dexter, believes Dexter was one of the wealthier members of the black community.

Dexter's obituary in the *Pennsylvania Gazette*, August 4, 1799, calls him "Noke Kinsey, a free African in the 70th year of his age." It goes on to say that he lived "almost thirty years in the family of John Pemberton in the capacity of coachman during which time he evinced such fidelity, tenderness, and honesty joined to an obliging temper as gained him the confidence and respect of all who knew him by his industry and care." It is unclear why he is referred to as "Noke Kinsey," a name that appears nowhere else in the written record. The manumission document calls him, "Oronoko Royal Slave" and elsewhere he is James Oronoco Dexter. According to research conducted by Dr. Daniel Rolph at the Historical Society of Pennsylvania, the name, Oronoco, was popular in

Abolitionist circles in the eighteenth century. It came from a short novel entitled *Oroonoko or, The Royal Slave in London*, by Aphra Behn, celebrated as one of the earliest female writers of fiction. The novel was published in 1688 and adapted into a play by Thomas Southerne in 1695. Southerne changed the plot slightly, and it is thought that his version got more attention than Behn's. In both versions, the enslaved Oronoco and his lover are banished from Africa to Surinam, an English colony in the Caribbean that would have been familiar to eighteenth-century Philadelphians.

We do not know what happened to Joseph Yeates after he left the Three Tun Tavern that became the Fountain Inn, but we do know how tavern culture changed. As the old egalitarian ways of drinking faded in the decade preceding the revolution, Anthony Fortune who apparently managed the Fountain

Figure 3.8. The Cross Keys Tavern, northeast corner of Chestnut and Third Streets. (Courtesy of Free Library of Philadelphia, Print and Picture Collection.)

Inn until 1775, moved on to manage an even larger establishment in the section of the city called Southwark. Bent on attracting an elite clientele, he called his new tavern the White Horse and described it as including "elegant and commodious buildings" as well as ample space for stabling horses. Joseph Ogden, who ran the One Tun Tavern (also called the Cross Keys) on the northeast corner of Third and Chestnut Streets, between 1767 and 1771, aimed to attract travelers (fig. 3.8). According to his tavern account book, which is in the Pennsylvania Historical Society, Ogden could squeeze in sixteen paying overnight guests and provide meals and stables for their horses. The brisk tavern business, however, still supported much smaller establishments, one of which left a record of its existence on Carter's Alley, at the site of the Museum of the American Revolution.

4

MRS. HUMPHREYS'S UNLICENSED TAVERN ON CARTER'S ALLEY, 1776–1783

AS I HOPE HAS ALREADY BECOME EVIDENT, archaeological stories begin with the artifacts. It is not that there is no documentary record, but the documentary record is often too minimal or too general to tell us much about what happened in a particular place at a particular time. The artifacts found in a privy associated with a property at No. 30 Carter's Alley are a prime example. More than a hundred liquor bottles were recovered from a layer of soil at the bottom of the privy, and Alex Bartlett, the archaeologist who analyzed them, thought they must have come from a tavern (fig. 4.1). The bottles were part of an assemblage of artifacts that dated to the 1770s and 1780s. We knew who lived on the property when they were thrown out, but we had not known they kept a tavern.

THE HUMPHREYS HOUSEHOLD

Benjamin and Mary Humphreys bought No. 30 Carter's Alley on July 10, 1776, just two days after the Declaration of Inde-

Figure 4.1. Liquor bottles from the Humphreys privy (feature 16). (Photograph by Juliette Gerhardt.)

pendence was read aloud in the State House yard, now Independence Square. They had previously lived on Chestnut Street between Fourth and Fifth Streets, where Benjamin made screws of all different sizes and sharpened sickles. In 1773, however, he decided to make a change, and on May 19 of that year he advertised his business for sale in the *Pennsylvania Gazette*:

> To be SOLD, by the SUBSCRIBER, at his house, in Chestnut Street, between Fourth and Fifth streets. . . . A complete ENGINE, for cutting clothiers, timber, packing, tobacco, and other SCREWS, from 1½ to 6 inches in diameter; likewise a MACHINE, accurately made for cutting BOXES to fit them: And, as the

subscriber intends to decline that business, he will undertake to instruct the purchaser, and make him fully acquainted with every particular relative to the ART of SCREW-CUTTING, so that he may not labour under any difficulty in carrying on the work to the greatest advantage.

In April and August of 1774 and August of 1775 Benjamin Humphreys was issued a tavern license, but that is his last recorded license. When he died almost twenty years later he was identified as a cutler, that is, a maker of screws, as he had been before.

It is possible that Benjamin and Mary Humphreys moved to Carter's Alley a year to two before they bought the property, because they requested a transfer from one Quaker monthly meeting to another in December 1775. The transfer was granted in May 1776, just two months before they bought the Carter's Alley property. No. 30 Carter's Alley was not technically within the southern meeting house district; but its location at Fourth and Chestnut Streets would have been more convenient than the Arch Street meeting house the Humphreys had previously attended. They transferred back to Arch Street, however, when the southern district meeting house moved to Pine and Second Streets in 1779.[1]

Attendance at Quaker meeting was a daily practice for many members. They were also expected to avoid excessive drinking of spirituous liquors, stay away from music houses, dancing, and gambling, take care of the poor, not indulge in gossip, and not be involved in the "importing or buying

---

1. The Humphreys requests are recorded in U.S. Quaker Meeting Records for 1775, 1774, and 1779.

of Negroes."[2] It is probably no coincidence that Benjamin Humphreys announced the release from bondage of a "Negro Woman named Quansheba aged about thirty-four years" in March of 1776, just a year after Quakers founded the Pennsylvania Abolition Society. Humphreys's notice in the monthly meeting minutes read, "Unto the said Negro Woman all my right, and all Claim whatsoever as to her person, or to any estate she may acquire hereby declaring the said Quansheba (also spelled 'Quasheba') absolutely free, without any interruption from me, or any person claiming under me." Quansheba may, however, have remained in the Humphreys household because his 1794 will directed that the "old Negro Woman Quasheba be maintained and supported out of my Estate during her Life."

AN UNLICENSED TAVERN

Otherwise we know little about Benjamin and Mary Humphreys. They did not have children, but a niece lived with them in 1784 and again with Mary for a year after Benjamin died. It is the artifacts from the privy that led us to more information about this seemingly upstanding Quaker family. Besides the alcohol bottles, there were eighteen tankards in regulation sizes (pint, half-pint, quarter-pint), thirty-eight drinking glasses of one kind or another, seven punch bowls, eight jugs, and three decanters (fig. 4.2). Taverns were strictly regulated in the Revolutionary period with the city setting prices for specific quantities of alcohol and services (Thompson 1999: 15–21). Besides the drinking vessels and bottles, other artifacts

---

2. Barbour and Frost 1988 examines the twelve queries that guided Quaker behavior as well as much more of Quaker practice and history.

Figure 4.2. Tavern artifacts including bottles and tankards in standard sizes from the Humphreys privy (feature 16). (Photograph by Juliette Gerhardt.)

found in the Humphreys privy resemble artifacts associated with taverns found elsewhere. These included twenty-nine slip-decorated pie dishes and chargers, thirteen teapots, six porringers, eleven bowls, and twenty-three chamber pots. The number of chamber pots is surely a sign that the assemblage represented something more than a single, childless household. Other possible tavern-related artifacts found on the site included buttons (107), snuff bottles (seven), and clay pipe fragments (seventy-three). Benjamin Humphreys listed himself as a "sometime past blacksmith, now innholder" on the deed for the Carter's Alley property, but no license for running a tavern could be found for any year after 1775. We looked everywhere.

I went through two volumes of a ledger of "licenses for marriages, taverns, and pedlars" at the Historical Society of Pennsylvania, and archaeologist Tod Benedict, who did much

MADE IN PHILADELPHIA—PORCELAIN

Part of a white ceramic punchbowl found at the bottom of the Humphreys privy stumped the archaeological team when they first saw it. Unlike white salt-glazed stoneware, which is common on an early eighteenth-century site, the bowl was translucent. Light seemed to pass through it, something light does not do with stoneware. It wasn't as white as Chinese porcelain, but it wasn't as creamy as earthenware either. Juliette Gerhardt, who analyzed the ceramics for the Museum of the American Revolution project, consulted Robert Hunter, another ceramics expert and editor of the journal Ceramics in America for the Chipstone Foundation. Hunter was equally mystified but suggested sending a sample sherd to J. Victor Owen, an expert on the geochemistry of archaeological ceramics and glass at St. Mary's University in Halifax, Nova Scotia. Owen's chemical analysis concluded that the bowl was high-grade porcelain, apparently made in Philadelphia. Hunter calls it the holy grail of ceramics, the first physical evidence of high-grade porcelain made in North America.

Above: Porcelain punch bowl attributed to Philadelphia potters Bonnin and Morris.

The most likely manufacturers of the bowl were Bonnin and Morris, whose American China Manufactory warehouse was located between Second and Front Streets not far north of the Museum of the American Revolution site. In 1967 and 1968 a portion of Bonnin and Morris's kiln site in the Southwark section of Philadelphia was excavated by Paul Huey and Garry Wheeler Stone, students of archaeologist John Cotter at the University of Pennsylvania, and the material recovered was analyzed by Graham Hood, then curator of the Yale University Art Gallery. The results of the excavation indicated that Bonnin and Morris were manufacturing soft-paste porcelain, but there was no evidence that they had figured out how to produce hard-paste porcelain. The difference between soft-paste and hard-paste porcelain is that soft-paste, also called bone china, is not translucent and is less like glass than hard paste, which is fired at a higher temperature.

Nineteen whole vessels made of soft-paste porcelain by Bonnin and Morris are known to exist and were exhibited at the Philadelphia Museum of Art in 2008. Bonnin and Morris were only in operation for two years, which means that the vessels had to have been made between 1770 and 1772. The factory may have tried to produce hard-paste porcelain during those years, but until the punchbowl was found on the Museum of the American Revolution site no examples were known to exist. In an article published in 2016, Robert Hunter and Juliette Gerhardt speculate that American potter Andrew Duché's arrival in Philadelphia in 1769 and the simultaneous arrival of a shipment of Carolina clay in 1770 likely contributed to Bonnin and Morris's successful production of true porcelain. Duché had discovered fine white clay in the 1730s along the Savannah River in western North Carolina, where it was valued by the Cherokee Indians for making clay pipes. He experimented with using it to make porcelain on and off during the next thirty years. He may well have brought his expertise back to Philadelphia and shared it with Bonnin and Morris.

Bonnin and Morris was the first and only American porcelain manufactory predating the Revolutionary War. That the factory produced the elusive hard-paste as well as soft-paste porcelain is evidence of the competence American manufacturing had reached even before independence. ∎

Much of the information presented here is drawn from Hunter and Gerhardt 2016.

of the research for the project, went through everything he could find at the city archives. He did not find a license or application for a license for a tavern at No. 30 Carter's Alley, but he did find a 1783 charge against Mary Humphreys for "keeping a disorderly house," a term that implied an unlicensed drinking establishment where prostitutes also plied their trade.[3] Even though she was declared "not guilty of the particulars charged in the bill," the judgment required that, "She be committed to the Gaol of this City till Saturday week next, and that on the said day She be carted through this City and that She be afterwards confined in the Workhouse at hard labour for three months, that She pay the Costs of this Prosecution, and stand committed, till this Sentence is completed with" (fig. 4.3). It seems a rather harsh punishment for a person declared not guilty of at least one of the charges against her, and no evidence tells us whether she actually served her sentence. Historian Peter Thompson notes that women were punished disproportionately more than men for keeping an illegal tavern. While women ran approximately a quarter of the city's taverns, nearly half the number of prosecutions for keeping illegal ones were brought against women (Thompson 1999: 45).

The tavern-related artifacts came from a privy that had been closed by 1789. We know this because a deed describes a "new necessary house" built on a small parcel of land that Benjamin Humphreys acquired from a neighbor in 1789. According to the deed, the "new necessary house" was located "about five feet seven inches thence westerly by the said old

---

3. The charge against Mary Humphreys was found in the Mayor's Court Dockets. Sharon Salinger (2002) describes Philadelphia's disorderly houses as typically including prostitutes (12).

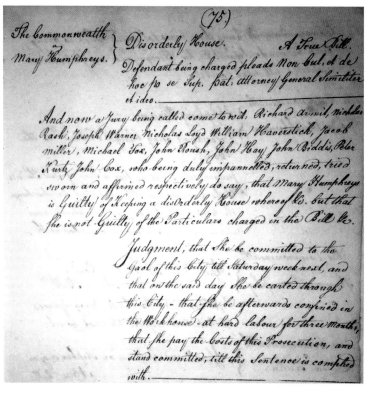

Figure 4.3. Charge against Mary Humphreys for keeping a disorderly house, Mayor's Court dockets, 1783.

necessary house now filled up."[4] Not surprisingly, the most recent manufacturing date (what archaeologists call a *terminus post quem*) for an artifact recovered from the "old necessary house" (our feature 16 on fig. 1.14) was 1780, but some of the artifacts had been made earlier, including a punchbowl found in fragments at the very bottom of the privy.

4. Deed recorded in the Philadelphia County Deed Book, D33, 182–183, 1789, on file at the Recorder of Deeds, Philadelphia.

The following short vignette weaves archaeological and historical data together to imagine what Mrs. Humphreys might have been thinking. It is a technique I have used elsewhere to bring the past to life and make sense of what we have found (Yamin 1998).

WEAVING IT ALL TOGETHER—MRS. HUMPHREYS

Mrs. Humphreys didn't want to bother her husband about tavern business, but she couldn't help herself. She was annoyed that the man had taken down her precious punch bowl from the shelf where it had sat forever and particularly annoyed that he had dropped it. Yes, it could be mended, but it would never be the same. She was sure he'd done it purposefully. He was a Loyalist, and he didn't care that the Tryphena had carried a message against the Stamp Act to Britain before the war. With his fancy clothes and fancy signet ring he was on the wrong side, and she wished he wouldn't even drink at her table— never mind the money she made off him. She didn't mind the other imbibers, who scratched their names and messages in the front windows—they, at least, were patriots—but the fancy man she did mind. Mrs. Humphreys's hardworking husband—a cutler by trade—told her to calm down. The war would soon be over, and they would hopefully not have to risk running the unlicensed tavern anymore. The caution came too late though. Mrs. Humphreys was charged in 1783 with "keeping a disorderly house," committed to the gaol of the city, carted through the streets, and confined to the workhouse at hard labor for three months. The broken punch bowl was the least of her worries. ∎

Above: Close-up of the mends to the punch bowl with the words "Success to the Tryphena" painted inside it.

THE TRYPHENA PUNCHBOWL

As soon as Kathryn Wood, who was carefully excavating feature 16, began to uncover the sherds of the punchbowl she knew it was special (fig. 4.4). They appeared to have the image of a ship on them with writing below the ship. The sherds were temporarily taped together while we were still in the field, and even though the bowl was far from complete, it was possible to decipher an elegantly painted two-masted ship with the words "Success to the Tryphena" beneath it. More sherds were found in the laboratory, and once they were all glued together the bowl was nearly complete (figs. 4.5 and 4.6). The design is not unique. Bowls wishing successful voyages were made to celebrate the launching of ships, and many were made in Liverpool, where it is likely the Tryphena bowl was made. Newspapers dating to the 1760s announce trips made by the Tryphena between Philadelphia and Liverpool. In 1763, for instance, the *Pennsylvania Gazette* announced that the Tryphena, under Captain John Smith, had arrived from Liverpool with a "large and neat assortment of goods, suitable for the season." Listed were all sorts of textiles: cotton Holland stripes, English sheeting, Manchester velvets, and Irish linen. In 1764 Captain Smith brought "a fresh assortment of choice 3–4, 7–8 and yard wide housewives cotton checks" and in 1765 he delivered goods to Philip Benezet's store in Market Street. In just one instance the newspapers reported what Smith carried to Liverpool. On October 2, 1766 the *Pennsylvania Gazette* published "A memorial from the merchants and Traders of this city, to the Merchants and manufacturers of Great Britain, praying them to interest themselves in endeavouring to get the Stamp Act repealed, and other regulations in our Trade, redressed, is now drawn up and signed, and it is to

Figure 4.4. Kathryn Wood and Kevin Bradley excavating the Humphreys privy (feature 16). (Photograph by Tim Mancl.)

be forwarded by the Tryphena, Capt. Smith for Liverpoole." The notice also ran in the *London Evening Post* on January 23–25, 1766, issue 5967.

We do not know why this bowl was among Benjamin and Mary Humphreys's possessions, although Captain Smith may have been a regular customer. We do not know if they were even aware of the message the Tryphena had carried to the merchants and manufacturers of Great Britain. Like many other Quakers, the Humphreys were likely pacifists and might have interpreted the message, if they even knew about it, as preventative. If Great Britain ceased to "tax without representation," war might be avoided. Or, they might have been as angry as many others at Great Britain for leveling taxes that made commerce too expensive. They were, after all, businesspeople. We do know the relevance of the message the Try-

Figure 4.5. The Tryphena punch bowl (interior) recovered from the Humphreys privy (feature 16). Made in Liverpool. (Photograph by Juliette Gerhardt.)

Figure 4.6. The Tryphena punch bowl (exterior) recovered from the Humphreys privy (feature 16). (Photograph by Juliette Gerhardt.)

phena carried to the site where it was found (now the location of a museum of the American Revolution): objections to the Stamp Act were, after all, one of the complaints that led to the war.

WRITING ON WINDOW PANES

Other artifacts with possible political significance were found in the Humphreys privy. While guiding the processing of artifacts in Commonwealth Heritage Group's laboratory, Juliette Gerhardt noticed words scratched into pieces of window glass. When the glass fragments were pieced together, the writing could be read. It included names of people who were probably patrons of the Humphreys tavern, but it also included a phrase from a famous political speech (fig. 4.7). The phrase reads, "We admire riches and are in love with i . . . [idleness]." Juliette traced the phrase to a speech that Roman senator Marcus Portius Cato (Cato the Younger) made to the Roman Senate in 63 BCE. According to her research, the speech referred to the fate of a group of conspirators who had plotted to overthrow the Republic. Cato was warning the senators against dissipation and laziness and encouraging them to be vigilant and active in the defense of the Roman Republic. As a member of the Stoic school of philosophy, Cato championed republicanism, virtue, and liberty. He opposed the tyranny of Julius Caesar, who had addressed the senate just before Cato, but was loyal to the state. Both Cato's speech and Julius Caesar's were recorded by the Roman historian Sallust, whose work was translated from the Latin by an English schoolmaster named John Clarke in 1734. The Scottish political writer and pamphleteer, Thomas Gordon, drew on the translations for his critiques of the British political system,

Dinnin

We admire riches
And are in love with i..[idleness]

Henry de Haas

WM

Figure 4.7. Window glass with names and phrase scratched into it. Recovered from the Humphreys privy (feature 16). (Photograph by Juliette Gerhardt.)

which were published in 1744 and were probably well known to the Founding Fathers.

A play called *Cato, A Tragedy* by John Addison popularized Cato's ideas about individual liberty versus government tyranny and corruption. It was a favorite of George Washington, who reportedly had it performed at Valley Forge. Historians have noted that many famous sentiments expressed in the American Revolution were inspired by the play. Among them were Nathan Hale's words, "I only regret I have but one life to give for my country," surely based on the line "What pity it is that we can die but once to serve our country" uttered in Act IV of the play (Lehrman Institute 2005–2017). Although the quote scratched on the Humphreys's window pane did not come from the play, it was put there by someone familiar with

Cato's philosophy. Whether he was referring to British tyranny and the Revolutionary cause or just showing off his knowledge we cannot know for sure, but the tavern context in this period was habitually political, and it would not be surprising if the message was meant as a criticism of British conduct.

Among those scratched in the glass, the name Henry de Haas appears in closest proximity to the Cato quote. A cooper named Henry Haas lived a few blocks away from the Humphreys tavern on North Third Street, and Brigadier General John Philip de Haas, who distinguished himself in the Revolution, lived on Third Street from 1779 until his death in 1786 (Dacus 2015). Either of them might have scratched the quote in the window pane although the names "Finley," "Dinnin," and "WM" were also scratched there. Macpherson's 1785 directory shows a blacksmith named Charles Finley living on Smith's Alley, around the corner from the Humphreys, and he may have been a regular. "Dinnin" couldn't be traced, but "WM" was most likely the initials of William McDougall, the dancing master (dance teacher) who lived next door to the Humphreys on Carter's Alley and sold them the small piece of land where they built the "new necessary" in 1789. It is tantalizing to think of the men who hoisted their tankards at the Humphreys's table and possibly marked their presence by scratching their names in window panes.

Another artifact found in the privy, this one the gemstone from a signet ring, complicates the story even more (fig. 4.8). The gem is carved with the British Royal Coat of Arms and may have been lost by a British gentleman. Even though this was the period when gentlemen and laborers supposedly chose to drink in separate spaces, the signet ring suggests otherwise. As is often the case, the archaeological evidence reveals a reality full of contradictions.

Figure 4.8. Signet ring gem with the British Coat of Arms carved into it. Recovered from the Humphreys privy (feature 16). (Photograph by Juliette Gerhardt.)

Mrs. Humphreys herself is a contradiction. While she may have been keeping an illegal tavern, she appears to have set an appropriately "simple" table for her family. Her dishes were plain but fashionable (fig. 4.9) and her teawares were positively elegant (fig. 4.10). In the event that she did serve time in jail and at hard labor, it does not seem to have hindered the rest of her life. She returned to No. 30 Carter's Alley and remained there until her death in 1822 at the ripe old age of ninety-two. She had outlived her husband by twenty-eight years. The neighborhood was in a state of transformation by the time Mary Humphreys died; commercial buildings were replacing residential ones, and the narrow lots that had been carved out of the original patents were about to be recombined to accommodate big buildings. The Humphreys residential household was one of the last on Carter's Alley.

Figure 4.9. Mrs. Humphreys's English-made creamware tableware set. (Photograph by Juliette Gerhardt.)

Figure 4.10. Mrs. Humphreys's English-made hand-painted tea set in the Blowsy Rose pattern. (Photograph by Juliette Gerhardt.)

5

DR. JAYNE'S SKYSCRAPER
AND THE TRANSFORMATION OF
THE NEIGHBORHOOD

A DEVASTATING FIRE consumed many buildings between Third Street, Goforth's Alley, and Dock Street in 1806. It was not the first in the neighborhood, but the newspaper accounts of this fire provide a good idea of how much more commercial Mrs. Humphreys's neighborhood had become by the first decade of the nineteenth century.[1] The fire, described in the papers as a "dreadful conflagration," started in the frame workshop of Joseph Burr, a Windsor chair and trunk maker, at the corner of Dock Street and Goforth's Alley. It spread west to Relief Alley and north to Carter's Alley (fig. 5.1). The two large brick houses next to Burr's on Goforth's Alley burned as did three frame houses on the east side of the alley and two brick houses at the corner of Carter's Alley. Mr. Ramage, a printer's joiner, had his shop in one of those houses, and another joiner kept shop in a frame building at

---

1. Newspapers recording the fire include the *Aurora General Advertiser*, the *New York Gazette*, and the *Public Ledger*.

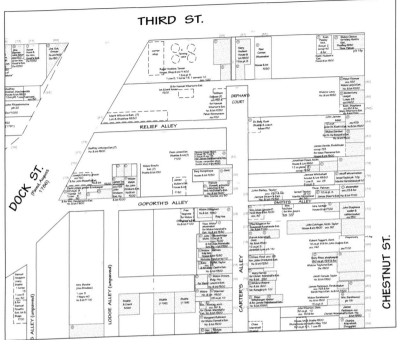

Figure 5.1. 1787 map reconstruction of Block 600 including the area between Goforth Alley and Third Street made by Anna Coxe Toogood for the National Park Service, 1985. (Courtesy of Independence National Historical Park.)

the southwest corner of Relief Alley. Printer's joiners made the supportive furniture for print shops. The prevalence of joiners' shops in the streets and alleys is a sure indicator of how important printing was to the neighborhood.

Shops affected by the fire along Relief Alley belonged to Oliphant and Wilson, upholsterers, Mr. Baldwin, a shoemaker, and Richard Coxley, a currier (leather processor). James Molony's house on the north side of Carter's Alley across from Relief Alley was damaged, and Mr. Bioren's print shop on the north side of the alley was destroyed. Four brick houses across from

United States Bank (now known as First Bank) including Mr. Dufar's counting house (business office) were damaged, and Mrs. Wetherall's brick house at the head of Carter's Alley and the frame blacksmith shop next door burned to the ground. Wood frame houses belonging to Joseph Burr and John Payne on the south side of Carter's Alley just to the east of South Third Street were also destroyed. It appears that Mrs. Humphreys's house at No. 30 Carter's Alley further to the east was spared, but her household was definitely affected. As of 1806, the records show that John Payne and his wife, Elizabeth, lived with Elizabeth's great aunt Mary Humphreys.

Elizabeth Payne eventually inherited and moved into her great aunt's property, but from at least 1806 until 1822 when Mary Humphreys died the two families shared a household. Elizabeth's husband, John, was a mariner, an occupation historian Billy G. Smith ranks among the lowest in terms of material standards, status, and occupational and economic mobility (Smith 1990: 4). There definitely would have been economic advantages to combining households, and there would have been an advantage for Mary Humphreys since she was seventy-six in 1806 and could probably have used some help. Elizabeth Payne's administration, made in 1834, lists "a sick man's chair" and a "patient bed and mattress" in the attic. Perhaps they were for her ailing great aunt in her last years.

CARTER'S ALLEY

Residents affected by the 1806 fire petitioned the city to open Carter's Alley to South Third Street to make the western end of the alley (shown as Orphan's Court in fig. 5.1) more accessible to firefighters. The petition was granted, and the alley was cut through a property that had originally belonged to the Hudson family, descendants of one of the block's earliest residents. Goforth's Alley was eventually widened along its full length, an action that cut off much of the property at its intersection with Chestnut Street. The owner of the corner property did not like his building being torn down to accommodate the road, and in 1833 he added in its place a four-foot-wide building nicknamed "Squeezegut Row" (Yamin et al. 2010: 22).

John Payne died the same year that Squeezegut Row was built, and Elizabeth died just a year later. She left her inherited property to her brother, William Winn, who rented it to Christopher Harper, a tavernkeeper next door at No. 28 Carter's Alley. Strictly residential occupation of Carter's Alley had clearly ended by the 1830s, and the artifacts left in the "new" privy at No. 30 may be its last evidence (fig. 5.2). The artifacts, though, are somewhat confusing since some probably belonged to Mrs. Humphreys, others to Elizabeth and John Payne, and still others to the tavern at No. 28 that by 1832 was physically connected to No. 30. A Mutual Assurance Company policy issued that year to Catherine Ann Harper for the southwest corner of Carter's and Goforth's Alleys describes "a neat Tavern Bar, Mahogany top," a new seven-by-nine-and-a-half-foot piazza, and doorways in each story that communicate with "a two story brick house on the west" that form "together one establishment."

The white dinnerware found in the privy was probably Mrs. Humphreys's since, other than the ware type (whiteware), the pattern was identical to the dishes she threw out in the 1780s (fig. 5.3). The teawares in the privy, which may or may not have been chosen by Mrs. Humphreys, differed and came in a variety of colors (figs. 5.4 and 5.5). The garish pink and black pieces in the Villa pattern, however, clearly

Figure 5.2. The "old" privy and the "new" privy on the Humphreys property at No. 30 Carter's Alley. (Photograph by Tim Mancl.)

Figure 5.3. Mrs. Humphreys's whiteware table set found in the "new" privy (feature 12). (Photograph by Juliette Gerhardt.)

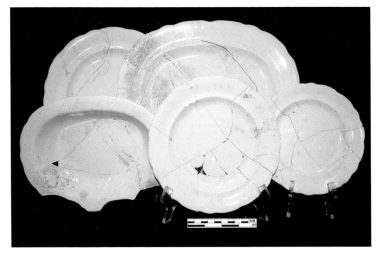

Figure 5.4. Dark blue transfer-printed teawares made in Staffordshire, England. London-shaped teapot with luster accents; miniature dish with Castle Garden Battery, New York design made by Enoch Wood, 1818–1846, and "Rebecca at the Well" cream jug. Found in the "new" (feature 12) privy. (Photograph by Juliette Gerhardt.)

Figure 5.5. Transfer-printed teawares made in Staffordshire, England. London-shaped black tea bowl and saucer with romantic print and pink luster sugar bowl in the British View series made by Enoch Wood, 1818–1846. Found in the "new" (feature 12) privy. (Photograph by Juliette Gerhardt.)

Figure 5.6. Pink and black transfer-printed table setting in the Villa pattern made in Staffordshire, England, by John Ridgway from 1830 to 1840. Possibly from the Harper Tavern. Found in the "new" (feature 12) privy. (Photograph by Juliette Gerhardt.)

reflect someone else's taste—maybe chosen by Elizabeth after her great aunt finally died or even used in the Harper tavern (fig. 5.6). Villa-patterned wares were not manufactured until 1830, that is, eight years after Mrs. Humphreys died and just four years before Elizabeth Payne died. Many (fifty-four) glass tumblers in the assemblage also clearly came from the tavern as well as a transfer-printed serving dish decorated with the "Texian Campaigne," an event that took place during the Texas Revolution in 1835–1836 (figs. 5.7 and 5.8). Elsewhere ceramics decorated with military motifs have been associat-

Figure 5.7. Well-worn glass tumblers probably from the Harper Tavern. Found in the "new" (feature 12) privy. (Photograph by Juliette Gerhardt.)

Figure 5.8. Transfer-printed serving dish showing the Texas campaign, which took place in 1835–1836. Pattern attributed to James Beech, active 1835 to 1844. Possibly from the Harper Tavern. (Photograph by Juliette Gerhardt.)

ed with brothels, perhaps because the motifs particularly appealed to men.[2] It would not be surprising if Harper's Tavern also served as a brothel or at the very least as an inn. Once combined with the house at No. 30, rooms would have been available for overnight guests.

While Mrs. Humphreys's illegal tavern at No. 30 Carter's Alley in the Revolutionary period was more or less hidden in a residential neighborhood, Mr. Harper's legal tavern was surrounded by other commercial establishments. The alley neighborhood had changed radically by the middle of the nineteenth century, but the Chestnut Street side of the Museum of the American Revolution block was even more dramatically changed.

THE JAYNE BUILDING

In 1849, Dr. David Jayne, a patent medicine manufacturer, demolished two shops in the middle of the Chestnut Street frontage where the Museum of the American Revolution now stands to make room for a building like no other in Philadelphia. It was made of solid granite; it rose eight stories above the street and was crowned with a two-story-high tower (fig. 5.9). While most of the buildings on this section of Chestnut Street were commercial by this time, none approached the scale of Dr. Jayne's. There was space for seeing patients, producing medicines and other products, selling "fancy goods," and printing the monthly publication, *Dr. D. Jayne's Medical Almanac and Guide to Health*. By 1857 wings had been added

---

2. Steve Brighton (2000), who analyzed the ceramics on the Five Points site in Lower Manhattan, suggested that the military themes found on dishes associated with a brothel were possibly chosen to please the clients.

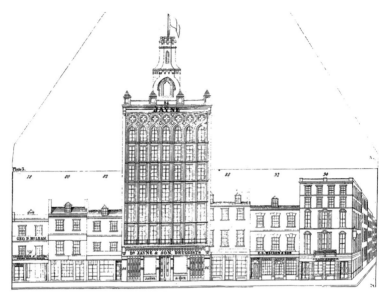

Figure 5.9. The Jayne Building, 1851. Panoramic line drawing of the south façade (Rae 1851). (Courtesy of Free Library of Philadelphia, Print and Picture Collection.)

to either side of the building, which extended all the way back to Carter's Alley, and by 1860 it was connected to another building south of the alley via a tunnel, the door to which was uncovered during the archaeological excavation (fig. 5.10). The most substantial finds associated with Dr. Jayne's building were huge granite blocks, some as much as eleven feet in length (fig. 5.11). Smaller finds included bottles for expectorant and vermifuge, products that promised to cure practically everything (fig. 5.12).

Figure 5.10. *(Facing page, side-turned)* Hexamer map showing the original Jayne Building, its added wings, the tunnel under Carter Street, and the extra building south of Carter Street. (Hexamer 1897, original on file at the Free Library of Philadelphia.)

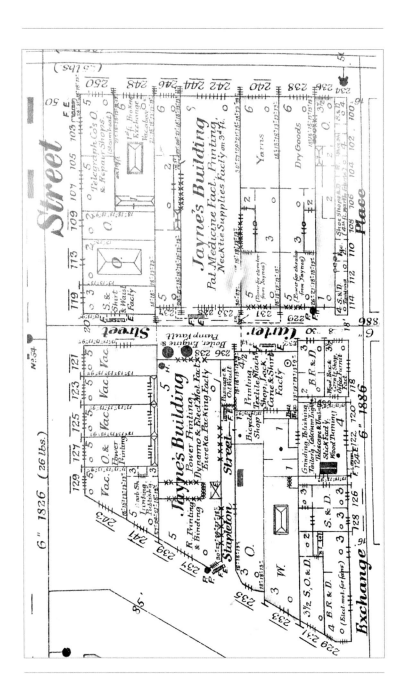

Figure 5.11. Jayne Building foundations uncovered in the excavation. (Photograph by Tim Mancl.)

Figure 5.12. Patent medicine bottles with Dr. Jayne labels found in the well next to the Jayne Building foundations. (Photograph by Juliette Gerhardt.)

Figure 5.13. Dr. Jayne's advertisement for Tonic Vermifuge and Expectorant (Knapp & Co. Lithographers 1889).

David Jayne was trained as a medical doctor at the University of Pennsylvania, but he marketed his "family medicines" to nonprofessionals as home remedies (fig. 5.13) (Ratini 2016).[3] At that he was enormously successful; he reportedly lived in a "great white marble mansion," and in 1857 was listed as one of Philadelphia's twenty-five millionaires. His building was clearly the expression of a man who craved attention and was ready to advertise his success. Sparing no expense, the building he constructed included 1,783 tons of Quincy granite, transported by water from Massachusetts. On September 6, 1850, the *Public Ledger* reported that "the last block of granite composing the cornice of the massive structure . . . was laid in the appropriate place yesterday thus completing the Chestnut Street front. . . . The Carter's Alley front has been delayed by the wreck of the vessel containing granite for two stories. This, however, has been replaced by duplicates, arrived from the quarries of Connecticut and the work will be resumed as soon as the repaving of Third Streets and Carter's Alley is completed." Note that construction involved more than the building itself. Streets had to be paved as well, presumably at Dr. Jayne's expense.

---

3. Research done by Meagan Ratini for Yamin et al. 2016 report. For further details, see Young 1961, Hechtlinger 1970, King (1902) 2012, and Geffen 1982.

The *Public Ledger* also mentions a "tall pole" in Chestnut Street that would have to be raised in Carter's Alley to lift the granite. A November 2, 1850, article noted that "the pole used by S.K. Hoxie in elevating the granite used in the construction of Dr. Jayne's building was yesterday brought down to a horizontal position, and now lies stretched along Carter's Alley." As described in Webster's 1828 *American Dictionary*, a *pole* was used to support scaffolding during construction and was typically made from the small-diameter trunk of a tall, straight tree. The granite, however, was put in place by the boom of a hoisting machine. S. K. Hoxie, the contractor for the project, was not the first to use a hoist for building construction, but he was the first to use a steam-powered hoist. His company—the Philadelphia Granite Company—also supplied the granite, and Hoxie and Mr. Collins, the rigger, were congratulated in a November 29 *Public Ledger* article for "the hoisting of the massive stones to their destined place" with no one hurt and no ropes or timbers broken. The building was supported by cast iron columns on each floor.

The interior of the building was also elaborate and designed to state-of-the art standards. The drugstore portion had a fifty-foot-long marble counter and a mosaic marble floor, a few pieces of which were found in the archaeological excavation. The building's architect, William J. Johnston, designed the shape of the roof to supply a catchment of rainwater to provide water pressure for a building too high to receive water from the Fairmount Water Works. As reported in the *Public Ledger*, this feature allowed each floor to have running water and toilet facilities. Johnston died prematurely at age thirty-eight in 1849, and the celebrated architect Thomas U. Walter oversaw final construction. Walter famously went on to design Girard College in Philadelphia and the dome of the U.S. capitol in Washington, DC.

On March 3, 1872, a fire consumed the Jayne Building. Neither the availability of water from the water tanks on the top floor nor what was described as "excessive plastering" between floors prevented the fire from spreading. Firefighting efforts on the outside left the building encased in ice, and, although its structure survived, damage was extensive. The turret burned off and was never replaced, the top floors were gutted and left open to the air, and the upper floors of the granite façade cracked and fell into Carter Street. The *Public Ledger* reported that the printing presses used to print Jayne's almanacs, as well as a large number of the almanacs, were destroyed. Losses to the building and to businesses within it, including the Jayne & Son Company, were estimated to exceed $140,000, a significant amount of money at the time. Enough of the building was left to rebuild, though, and it continued to dominate the Chestnut Street frontage between Second and Third Streets until 1958 when the National Park Service took it down.

Charles Peterson, an architect working for the Park Service when Independence National Historical Park was created in the 1950s, tried to save the Jayne Building. Even before Peterson came to Independence Park he was a champion of historic preservation and among other things had created the Historic American Buildings Survey. He had the Jayne Building recorded and argued that it should be preserved as "one of Chestnut Street's monuments to American History." Peterson believed the building was nothing less than the prototype skyscraper and probably the crude model for the steel-framed skyscraper (the Wainwright Building) that Dankman Adler and Louis Sullivan designed forty years later in St. Louis.

Sullivan would have been familiar with the Jayne Building since he had worked for the architect Frank Furness, whose office was across the street from the building. The National Park Service, however, was trying to develop a historic core for the story of American independence. Along with other monumental structures built in the nineteenth century, the Jayne Building did not fit that vision, and it was sacrificed for the sake of creating an eighteenth-century landscape. Peterson had lost the battle.

Finding remnants of the Jayne Building archaeologically and throughout the construction site provided an opportunity to remember the building, its monumentality, and its champion. The museum had hoped to place one of the granite blocks found on the site in front of its new building, but there was no place big enough to store it on the site during construction. Some of the granite was instead delivered to University City in west Philadelphia to be used in small parks in the area.

BECOMING A CITY

Cities are always in a state of change. One of the great things about urban archaeology is that it provides a record of some of that change—a kind of window into the dynamics of the urban process. Even without standing structures, the archaeological investigation of the Museum of the American Revolution site revealed what happened to William Penn's eighteenth-century "green country town" in the process of becoming a nineteenth-century city. Most importantly, the excavation and its analysis introduced us to some of the ordinary people who played a part in the process. Mrs. Humphreys and Dr. Jayne probably would not have crossed paths even if they had lived on the block at the same time, but they both made an impact.

Their lives and work were part of what was happening all over the city of Philadelphia in the nineteenth century. Narrow alleys were widened into streets; mixed residential-commercial structures were replaced with multistory commercial ones; the landscape of low-rise buildings gave way to a skyline of high-rises. As people died their properties were subsumed by nearby businesses, and the congeniality of neighbors was replaced with the impersonal relationships of businesspeople.

The block was a less-than-desirable place to live after the middle of the nineteenth century—too crowded and too commercial. But it was a fine place to work, and the site left an archaeological record of that too. Printing businesses had arrived on the block by the last decade of the eighteenth century, and printing remained prominent into the second half of the nineteenth century. Dr. Jayne published an almanac to promote his patent medicine business, but magazines, newspapers, and even bibles were being published all around him. Once Dr. Jayne went out of business, his monumental Chestnut Street building was used for a completely different industry, which left so much evidence behind that we were able to give some of it away—not normal archaeological practice.

6

EVIDENCE OF INDUSTRY—PRINTING AND MANUFACTURING BUTTONS

AMONG THE FIRST ARTIFACTS FOUND on the Museum of the American Revolution site were pieces of printer's type. They were mixed in with a deposit of fragmentary artifacts dating to the late eighteenth century found next to a wall that appeared to crosscut Carter's Alley (fig. 6.1). The wall was later interpreted as part of the tunnel that led from the main part of the Jayne Building on Chestnut Street to its extension on the south side of Carter's Alley. The artifacts, including the printer's type, had apparently been disturbed during construction of the tunnel.

The presence of printer's type in Carter's Alley makes perfectly good sense. According to historical sources, printers, publishers, booksellers, and other associated craftsmen had begun to open shops in the Carter's Alley neighborhood by the last decade of the eighteenth century. Between 1790 and 1800, printers, printers' joiners, and paper manufacturers occupied ten structures on the Museum of the American Revolution site. Among them were Zachariah Poulson, Jr., who

Figure 6.1. Printer's type and eighteenth-century artifacts found in the vicinity of Bioren's shop. (Photograph by Tim Mancl.)

in 1791 began his printing business at No. 31 Carter's Alley, just across the alley from the Humphreys household. In later years he moved to 106 Chestnut Street where he published *Poulson's Advertiser*, one of the nineteenth-century's most successful (and oldest) daily newspapers (Bradley 2016). Adam Ramage, a printer's joiner, suffered damages to his shop on Goforth's Alley in the 1806 fire and later moved to the southwest corner of Relief and Carter's Alley, just a few doors to the west of Mrs. Humphreys. Ramage revolutionized printing with a new and improved cast iron press that was produced at the Evan's Mars Iron Works in Philadelphia (Richardson 1982: 247). John Bioren's print shop was located even further to the west on the north side of the alley, and we suspect that the print type found in the excavation had belonged to Bioren.

John Bioren is listed in city directories at No. 88 Chestnut Street from 1801 to 1820, but his shop was at the back of the property at No. 39 Carter's Alley. He was identified in the directories as a printer and bookseller and was a figure in the Philadelphia publishing world for forty years (Carson and Swan 1949). After apprenticing to Thomas Bradford, Bioren joined the firm of Mountford, Bioren and Co. which within a year had become Bioren and Madan. In 1795 Bioren and Madan published the first three volumes of the works of Shakespeare, the first edition to be published in the United States; in 1796, they published the last five volumes. "The works," Bioren stated, "would be printed on fine American paper in the stile [sic] of Typographical Elegance that shall reflect the highest credit to the American press." Bioren's partnership with Madan did not last, but he went on to publish many important works by himself including the actor James Fennell's autobiography, entitled *Apology*; Dr. Benjamin Smith Barton's *New Views of the Tribes and Nations of America*; a play by Charles Kimbel entitled "Plot and Counterplot or a Portrait of Cervantes . . . as performed at the Philadelphia Theatre;" various pamphlets, programs, checks for the Bank of the United States and the Bank of Pennsylvania; and even medicine bottle labels. He also worked with other Philadelphia printers, like Matthew Carey; Bioren contributed pages for the Carey Bible, the first Roman Catholic bible printed in the United States. With Carey, and later by himself, Bioren printed numerous multivolume versions of the laws of the state of Pennsylvania. He used his own type (perhaps the type found at the site) and made his own inks. According to two scholars who published an article about Bioren in the *Papers of the Biographical Society* in 1949, "Bioren's shop was frequented by patrons of the arts, businessmen, men of science, and politicians of the anti-Federalist persuasion." They suspected that Mr. Bioren was a Jeffersonian.

Bioren had disappeared from Carter's Alley by 1821, but two other publications, which appeared on the alley a little later, lasted into the twenty-first century. The *Pennsylvania Inquirer*, later the *Philadelphia Inquirer*, was published by Jesper Harding at 36 Carter's Alley beginning in 1829. As the paper became more successful, Harding moved it to a new iron and glass building at the southeast corner of Carter's Alley and South Third Street (No. 59 South Third). The *Saturday Evening Post* was published out of the *Inquirer*'s old quarters at No. 36 Carter's Alley until it, too, moved to South Third Street, in this case to the west side next to the Bank of the United States (First Bank) in 1840. The *Saturday Evening Post*, which still publishes six times a year, remained on South Third Street until the early twentieth century, when it moved to the elegant building of its publisher (Curtis) at the corner of Sixth and Walnut Streets. The *Philadelphia Inquirer* vacated South Third sooner but left evidence of its presence behind.

ARCHAEOLOGY AND THE *PHILADELPHIA INQUIRER*

The *Philadelphia Inquirer* was published at No. 59 South Third Street from 1834 to 1863. Jesper Harding bought the paper, originally called the *Pennsylvania Inquirer* in 1829, six months after it had been founded. In a successful maneuver to increase the paper's readership in 1840, Harding managed to get the rights to serialize two of Charles Dickens's early novels, *Barnaby Rudge* and *Master Humphrey's Clock*. It was Harding's son William, however, who really increased the paper's circulation. Taking over in 1856, William changed the name of the paper from the *Pennsylvania Inquirer* to the *Philadelphia*

Figure 6.2. Printer's type found in a privy shaft (feature 36) at No. 59 S. Third Street, the location of an early office of the *Philadelphia Inquirer*. (Photograph by Juliette Gerhardt.)

Inquirer and increased the paper's circulation from seven thousand in 1859 to seventy thousand by 1863. This huge increase had everything to do with the paper's coverage of the Civil War. Harding hired war correspondents, who kept the public abreast of developments and even informed the troops on both sides of what was happening. Reportedly it was not uncommon for twenty-five thousand to thirty thousand copies of an issue to be distributed among the soldiers.

The largest number of pieces of printer's type found on the Museum of the American Revolution site came from a privy shaft on the property where the *Inquirer*'s offices were located until 1863. While there were not enough pieces of printer's type from the location of Bioren's shop to analyze, seven hundred were found in the privy at No. 59 South Third Street (121 S. Third after consolidation in 1850), and twelve more were found in a second privy shaft on the property (fig. 6.2). A historical-archaeological study of printer's type from the Green print shop in Annapolis, Maryland, provided a model of what could be learned from printer's type. Archaeologist Kevin Bradley (2016), who helped excavate and did most of the mapping of the Museum of the American Revolution site, undertook a similar study for the museum project.[1]

The sample at Annapolis was much larger (eleven thousand pieces) than that found on the museum site, but certain measurable features were common to both: body size, height to paper, and the number and placement of nicks. Pieces of type used together had to be identical in body size and height to paper or the product would not print correctly. Nicks were added during molding to help printers verify that all pieces of type were from the same set and were facing the same direction. Sorting type by these features gives at least a conservative idea of the number of sizes employed (or, at the least, discarded) by the printer. If the same sizes appeared in the pages of a historical newspaper or other publication known to be published in the Carter's Alley neighborhood, at least a loose connection could be made between the recovered artifacts and printers who formerly operated along Carter's Alley.

The pieces of printer's type taken from the privy with the richest deposit (feature 36 on fig. 1.14) were measured and sorted by size, number, and placement of nicks. Out of 697 pieces, eight sizes were represented. The pieces were first measured in millimeters (mm) and then converted to the more commonly used point system to determine type size. The smallest print type present was Diamond, measuring roughly 1.5 mm or 4.5 points (pts) in body size. Pearl (5 pts), Agate (5.5

---

1. For further discussion of the Green print shop study, see Leone 2005: 111–51 and Little 1992: 85–94.

pts), Minion (7 pts), Brevier (8 pts), Bourgeois (9 pts), Long Primer (10 pts), and Small Pica (11 pts) were also present. The only size missing in the sequential order of known print type at the time was the 6-point Nonpareil, which curiously was also absent from the Annapolis collection.

In total, 25 percent of the printer's type from feature 36 was either broken or unidentifiable. Of the identified sizes, Small Pica represented 35 percent, the highest proportion of type in the collection. Long Primer, Minion, and Brevier represented 20, 11, and 6 percent of the type sizes, respectively, and Pearl and Diamond were also identified in relatively small amounts. A big difference between the type from the museum site and the type from Annapolis was the far greater percentage of the Bourgeois size in the Annapolis sample. Another notable difference was the presence of sizes greater than Small Pica in Annapolis, especially English. These larger sizes were absent from feature 36.

Melvil Dewey, a New York State library instructor and inventor of the Dewey decimal system, conducted a study on print type at the beginning of the twentieth century. He claimed that Pica (meaning Small Pica) was "the great standard" for newspaper work. He also noted that printers typically attempted to maximize the number of words on a page, especially in advertisements, and therefore used smaller sizes such as Long Primer and Bourgeois. The large percentages of Small Pica and Long Primer in feature 36 as well as the presence of smaller sizes such as Diamond, Pearl, and Brevier are consistent with printing a newspaper. The lack of large type sizes in feature 36, however, is perplexing. Even if the type collection indicates the production of a newspaper, presumably larger sizes such as Great Primer and Double Pica would have been needed for headlines and subtitles. Bradley speculated that

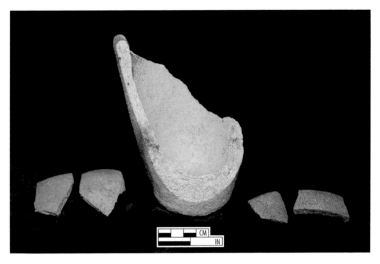

Figure 6.3. Crucible fragments probably used in the founding of printer's type for the *Philadelphia Inquirer*. (Photograph by Juliette Gerhardt.)

larger sizes would have been used less frequently and therefore discarded less frequently.

It seems reasonable to conclude that the type analyzed was used for printing a newspaper and represents remnants of the *Philadelphia Inquirer*'s occupation of the site. The *terminus post quem* of the feature (1867) was almost exactly contemporaneous with the removal of the *Inquirer*'s office from South Third Street, suggesting that the shaft was filled with material the paper left behind when moving out or when the new tenants moved in.

Five crude ceramic sherds from two crucibles (fig. 6.3) were found along with the printer's type. Crucibles are thick ceramic vessels designed to hold molten metal. They were used in type founding, a process of melting lead to a liquid state so it can be poured into molds to create the printer's type; the people who did this work were called type founders. According to McElroy's 1850 city directory, the *Philadelphia Inquirer* employed a type founder by the name of John Binny for a time. John's father, Archibald, was also a type founder and had been involved in the very beginnings of the American type-founding industry in Philadelphia in the late eighteenth century.

MR. LIPPINCOTT'S BUTTON FACTORY

While printer's type was among the first artifacts found on the Museum of the American Revolution site, button-manufacturing debris was among the last and most numerous. Tens of thousands of shell wasters and discarded blanks covered the subbasement floor of the central portion of the Jayne Building in the middle of the site (fig. 6.4). A grinding stone and the remains of a machine platform suggested that at least some manufacturing had taken place in Dr. Jayne's former basement. Industrial archaeologist Tim Mancl (2016) analyzed the button

Figure 6.4. Grinding wheel and shell wasters recovered from the subbasement of the central portion of the Jayne Building. (Photograph by Tim Mancl.)

debris, putting it in the context of what is known about the ocean shell button industry in the United States at the turn of the twentieth century.

Shell buttons manufactured in the United States were being made from both freshwater and ocean shells. The freshwater shells came mainly from the Mississippi River and its tributaries, while the ocean shells came from the South Pacific. The freshwater button industry in the United States was centered in Muscatine, Iowa, where mussel shell was the prime source of raw material. The ocean shell button industry, which was begun in the latter part of the nineteenth century by immigrants from the Bohemian region of what is now the Czech Republic, primarily used green turban and abalone shell. The ocean shell button industry was centered in New York City, but between the two world wars, the majority of ocean shell button blanks were produced in Milton, Delaware, and the surrounding area.

George Lippincott opened a button factory on Ionic Street (the former Carter Street, originally Carter's Alley) in 1913. The factory operated out of two buildings, one at 236–238 Ionic Street, the former location of Dr. Jayne's building south of Carter Street, and the other on Dock Street still further south. Lippincott made pearl buttons in Philadelphia out of green turban and abalone shells. He was not the only mother-of-pearl button manufacturer in Philadelphia. Another company listed in the 1919 *Third Industrial Directory of Philadelphia* was called the Kensington Pearl Button Company, and the directory also listed fifteen other button manufacturers. At least one of them (Emil Wahl Manufacturing), however, specialized in bone buttons, and still others may have made metal buttons. By 1922 the number of button manufacturers in Philadelphia had decreased to fourteen, but Lippin-

Figure 6.5. Inside the Lippincott Button Factory, Milton, Delaware. (Courtesy of the Delaware Public Archives.)

cott seems to have been thriving. In 1916 eighty-four people worked in his Philadelphia factory, two-thirds of them men; by 1922 the workforce had grown to 144. Children under fifteen accounted for only one in 1916 and five (three boys and two girls) in 1922. By then 72 percent of the workers were male.

Lippincott also owned a button factory in Milton, Delaware, sometime near the end of World War I, in the very area where sources say the majority of ocean shell button blanks were produced. That factory employed more than one hundred workers, and possibly as many as 168 (fig. 6.5). Lippincott was clearly an ambitious and inventive man. He patented at least three improvements to the manufacture of shell buttons, one that provided a method and means by which a maximum number of button blanks could be cut from a single shell without employing skilled labor. The two other patents were for devices that split the blank using a knife and rotary table instead of the hammer and chisel that were used when the blank was made by hand. Lippincott also produced a plant fertilizer called Plant Health out of shell that was not usable for buttons.

As described by Mancl, the first step in the manufacture of pearl buttons is soaking the shell to make it less brittle. Blanks are then cut from the shell and split, enabling more than one button to be made from the blank. Blanks were cut one at a time on a simple lathe. In a factory setting, the lathes were set in a line along the factory floor. The worker placed a shell against a stop, then, using a handle, drove a rotating tubular saw into the shell, producing a blank. Splitting the blank was done by skilled workers, a step that Lippincott hoped to eliminate with his invention. The split blanks were sorted by thickness and then sent for finishing, which involved drilling holes and polishing.

The button debris recovered archaeologically on the Museum of the American Revolution site mainly included "wasters" that did not meet the criteria for making buttons. For use in button making, the section of shell had to have a grain that ran parallel to the surface and no excessive curvature. Although the majority of the wasters found did not meet these criteria, they could still be measured to give an idea of what size buttons the Lippincott factory was attempting to make. Four five-gallon bucketfuls of wasters were recovered for analysis.

The waste materials made clear that the factory aimed to obtain the maximum number of blanks per shell. Blanks were cut in close proximity to one another and in a uniform manner. Examples show that blanks of different diameters were cut from the same piece to make the greatest use of available material. The diameter of blanks both in millimeters and lignes (the industry standard) was measured and indicated that buttons of different sizes and function were being produced including the following: shirt collar, probable sleeve, shirt placket (or front of the shirt), pant-pocket closure, and suit jacket closure. The highest percentage of measurable buttons (twenty-three out of thirty-one or 74 percent) was made for the fronts of shirts. It was also evident from the wasters that despite making efficient use of the shell for buttons, a considerable portion of shell was not usable, which likely explains Lippincott's attempt to market a fertilizer made from the leftovers.

CHANGE ABOVEGROUND AND ENDURANCE BELOW

Mr. Lippincott's Philadelphia button factory probably closed at the onset of the Second World War, which disrupted the availability of shell from the South Pacific. The National Park Service acquired the site soon after the war and, as already described, demolished the standing structures as part of the development of Independence National Historical Park. When they finally got around to building the visitor center in the 1970s, construction workers found shell debris and buttons in what they assumed was an old elevator shaft (fig. 6.6). There was no formal archaeological excavation, though, and the long record of physical change on the site was left untouched until 2014. That physical record, including about eighty-two thousand artifacts as well as building foundations and privy shafts dating to different periods, tells the general story of how American cities changed over time and the particular story

Figure 6.6. Button debris recovered during construction of the National Park Service Visitor Center in 1974.

of how one neighborhood in the oldest part of Philadelphia changed from the city's very beginnings up to the present. While the artifacts found are interesting in themselves, it is the people whose possessions they were that connect us to the lived past. It is historical archaeology's mission to do justice to those people who are, for the most part, unknown to history. Plenty is known about famous people in Philadelphia's past; it is some of the unfamous ones that we celebrate here.

7

PEOPLE FROM PHILADELPHIA'S PAST AND THE MAKING OF A MUSEUM

THE THINGS WE LEARN from historical archaeology are different than the things we learn from history alone. The most obvious difference is the people we meet. They are generally people who have not left written records of their lives, who, except for their names on documents such as deeds or death records, are unknown to history. Looking into their lives allows us at least a glimpse of what everyday life was like in different periods in particular places, in this case Philadelphia.

Some of the people we met on the Museum of the American Revolution site were anonymous—the probably German tanyard worker who lived on an alley at the eastern edge of the site in the early years of the eighteenth century, for instance—but others had names. William Carter, the man who owned the land where the tanner lived, was an early mayor of Philadelphia, and William Smith, the man who bought Carter's property in 1749, was a well-to-do tanner. He apparently curled his wig and sipped tea from fancy Chinese porcelain. His three sons managed the upkeep and sale of their father's property after his death; they paid his debts and hired local men to make improvements. They even appear to have invited the tavern keeper across the street to throw away his old inexpensive but colorful dishes after the tavern was renovated to cater to a more gentlemanly clientele.

The tavern keeper's name was Joseph Yeates. Besides learning what kinds of dishes and drinking vessels he used, we learned that he employed an enslaved African named James Oronoco Dexter and contributed to the cost of Dexter's manumission in 1768. Dexter, it turned out, became a leader in the African American community once he was free. He signed the petition to fence in a portion of Washington Square (known in the eighteenth century as Southeast Square) as a burial ground for the African community, and he was intimately involved with the founding of St. Thomas's African Episcopal Church in 1794.

Yeates's tavern was on Chestnut Street, a major artery leading down to the docks in the middle decades of the eighteenth century, but there were other taverns in less conspicuous places. Mary Humphreys kept an unlicensed tavern on Carter's Alley in the 1770s and 1780s. We learned quite a lot about her since she was arrested for keeping what was called "a disorderly house" and sent to gaol (jail) for a week and hard labor for three months. Whether or not she served her time we do not know, but we do know that she survived another forty years, living her last years with her grandniece Elizabeth Payne and her mariner husband at the same address where she had kept her disorderly house.

The Humphreys household was interesting in another way. When Mary and her husband, Benjamin, first moved to Carter's Alley, their household included an enslaved woman named Quansheba. Quaker records show that Benjamin

Humphreys manumitted Quansheba in 1776, but his will, which dates to 1794, specifies that Quansheba be "maintained and supported . . . during her life." Unlike James Oronoco Dexter, who left Yeates's employ as soon as he was free, Quansheba may have remained in the Humphreys household or at least nearby. Benjamin Humphreys was a cutler, and we learned things about him too. Like men in our own time, he seems to have had a kind of midlife crisis in his forties. He put the equipment he used for making screws up for sale and seemed to be trying to get rid of everything else (scythes and sickles) he had manufactured to change occupations. He moved his family to a new address on Carter's Alley, called himself an "inn keeper" on the deed, and got a tavern license for a single year. It was his wife, Mary, however, who kept the tavern.

We learned the names of many artisans and shopkeepers who worked on the site in the nineteenth century, but the most colorful was Dr. David Jayne, the patent medicine manufacturer who in the middle of the century built a headquarters on Chestnut Street that towered over everything that had been there before. Jayne was a millionaire, famous in his time, but virtually forgotten soon after. Even his prototype skyscraper was not considered worth saving when the National Park Service created Independence National Historical Park in the 1950s. Dr. Jayne's story demonstrates that even the rich can be forgotten. Archaeology uncovers what is there. Everything we find counts, and all of it contributes to bringing the past to life.

We met more people from the past on the Museum of the American Revolution site—William Harding, for instance, who made the *Philadelphia Inquirer* into a newspaper that has lasted to the present, and George Lippincott, whose button

manufacturing process produced shell debris that sits on cura-
tors' desks in the museum. This is not, however, the only site in
Philadelphia where archaeology has rediscovered people from
the past. The work done in association with the rejuvenation
of Independence Mall in the late 1990s and the first decade
of the twenty-first century introduced us to many early Philadelphians. The sites of planned new buildings on the three
blocks that make up the mall were all excavated: the Liberty
Bell and Independence Visitor Center sites by John Milner
Associates and the Constitution Center site by Kise, Straw, and
Kolodner. John Milner Associates found six privies on the Liberty Bell site and five on the visitor center site, but Kise, Straw,
and Kolodner, in conjunction with the National Park Service,
found 135 shafts of one kind or another on the Constitution
Center site. Most of them overflowed with artifacts, keeping
many archaeologists busy for many years.

Besides James Oronoco Dexter, another free African
American, Israel Burgoe, lived on the block where the Constitution Center now stands. Burgoe, a wood sawyer, and his
family's small house stood at the back of a lot owned by a
Quaker teacher named Benjamin Cathrall. Artifacts from
both Burgoe's and Cathrall's households were found in the
privy on the property, among them a wine bottle with Cathrall's seal on it and a collection of ceramic gaming pieces
similar to gaming pieces found elsewhere on sites associated
with African Americans. Caleb Cresson, a prominent Quaker
who was responsible for much of the early development of
the eastern portion of the Constitution Center block, left four
privies on properties that had belonged to him and also left a
journal that is now in the Historical Society of Pennsylvania.
One of the great advantages of historical archaeology is that
the things people leave behind provide an unintended record

of their lives—their tastes, their choices, their interests, their economic wherewithal—and the written record, when there is one, supplements our knowledge of them.

The Independence Visitor Center on the middle block of Independence Mall was my first major excavation in Philadelphia, and one of the privies on the site led us to one of my favorite people. William Simmons was a principal clerk in the auditor's office of the first Department of Treasury during George Washington's administration and later the chief accountant in the War Department. The unintentional record of his life, including lots of wine bottles and smoking pipes, suggested the conviviality of sharing his residence with politician boarders when congress was in session during the 1790s. Written letters I came across in Alexander Hamilton's published papers, however, revealed a curmudgeonly character who complained bitterly about the special treatment James McHenry, the head of the War Department, wanted Simmons to give to officers during his tenure in the department. His personality aside, Simmons is a reminder of the many bureaucrats who did the work of the first two administrations of the United States federal government. Their bosses—the Founding Fathers—are famous; the bureaucrats are mainly forgotten.

There was also a large cesspool on the middle block that belonged to two generations of the Everly family, comb makers and keepers of a dry goods emporium on Market Street in the 1830s and 1840s. Besides indications of upwardly mobile pretensions (fancy teawares and matching sets of dishes), the artifacts included lots of comb fragments and a roach trap, presumably used to keep the emporium presentable for customers.

Perhaps the most celebrated example of using archaeology to bring to light figures previously overlooked in Philadelphia history was found on the first block of Independence Mall where the Liberty Bell Center now stands. In 2007 the site of the house where George Washington lived while serving as the nation's first president was excavated. The purpose was to uncover what, if anything, remained of the house's foundations, especially the foundations associated with possible slave quarters at the back of the property. It had become widely known that nine enslaved Africans were part of the Washington household, and the African American community, in particular, wanted to know if anything remained of their presence. The excavation found no evidence of slave quarters, but a corner of the kitchen where many of the slaves worked was uncovered, albeit beneath foundations of buildings that stood on the property in the nineteenth century. Though fragmentary, the corner provided an emotional connection to the reality of the slave experience. Thousands of visitors stood on the platform that the Park Service built above the ongoing excavation and discussed the implications of slavery in the past and in the present.

While few sites are as dramatic as what is now called the President's House site, it illustrates the powerful connection with the past that archaeology creates. On the Museum of the American Revolution site, the connection is mainly made through artifacts, but its location is significant as well. Completed in 1797, the First Bank of the United States—Alexander Hamilton's bank—loomed over the site (fig. 7.1). Mary Humphreys and the Paynes would have watched its construction. Dr. Jayne undoubtedly would have bemoaned its old-fashioned style. The bank survives, and hopefully always will. The people who lived in its shadow, and those who came before, are remembered through the work of archaeologists across the street.

Figure 7.1. The Museum of the American Revolution site during excavation with the First Bank in the background on the opposite side of Third Street. (Photograph by Tim Mancl.)

THE HISTORY OF PHILADELPHIA
IN MICROCOSM

The excavation of the site of the Museum of the American Revolution revealed an unusually long view of the past. The earliest remains date to the turn of the eighteenth century and the most recent to a factory that operated in the early twentieth century. All places have a history, but not all places have a buried record of the past that touches on as many significant changes in a city's development. Although far from complete, the archaeological record reveals the history of Philadelphia in microcosm.

We often do not think of the recent past as part of history, but of course it is. The National Park's visitor center, which stood on the site before the museum was built, represents another episode in the site's long history. The building, which did not have a basement, protected the buried remains of earlier times, and the new museum will protect at least some of the remains that were recovered. The Tryphena punch bowl from the Humphreys house is displayed in one of the galleries, and many other artifacts are being used in the museum's educational program.

It seems particularly appropriate that a museum now stands on a site with such a deep historical record. While the museum is dedicated to the Revolution, it is also a place to tell stories of the people who once occupied its site and to cherish their possessions as links to the past.

REFERENCES

Barbour, Hugh, and J. William Frost. 1988. *The Quakers.* Richmond, IN: Friends United.

Benedict, Tod L. 2004. "Bricklayers, Well Diggers, Hod Carriers, Privy Cleaners, and Carters: The Construction and Maintenance of Brick-Lined Shafts in Philadelphia to 1850." Appendix B in *After the Revolution—Two Shops on South Sixth Street: Archeological Data Recovery on Block 1 of Independence Mall*, edited by Rebecca Yamin. Prepared for the National Park Service. John Milner Associates, Inc.

Bradley, Kevin C. 2016. "Printers and Printing along Carter's Alley." In *Archaeology of the City—The Museum of the American Revolution Site. Archaeological Data Recovery, Third and Chestnut Streets, Philadelphia Pennsylvania*, edited by Rebecca Yamin, 108–127. Submitted to the Museum of the American Revolution. Commonwealth Heritage Group. On file at Independence National Historical Park Library, Philadelphia.

Brighton, Stephen. 2000. "The Evolution of Ceramic Production and Distribution as Viewed from Five Points." Appendix B in *A Narrative History and Archeology of Block 160*, edited by Rebecca Yamin. Vol. 1 of *Tales of Five Points: Working-Class Life in Nineteenth-Century New York*, edited by Rebecca Yamin. West Chester, PA: John Milner Associates.

Bronner, Edwin B. 1982. "Village into Town, 1701–1746." In *Philadelphia, A 300-Year History*, edited by Russell F. Weigley. New York: W. W. Norton.

Carson, Marian S., and Marshall W. S. Swan. 1949. "John Bioren: Printer." *Papers of the Biographical Society* 43, no. 3.

Dacus, Jeff. 2015. "Brigadier General John de Haas: A Bad Example to Others." *Journal of the American Revolution* (April). Available at https://allthingsliberty.com/author/Jeff-Dacus.

Geffen, Elizabeth M. 1982. "Industrial Development and Social Crisis 1841–1854." In *Philadelphia: A 300-Year History*, edited by Russell F. Weigley, 307–362. New York: W. W. Norton.

Gerhardt, Juliette. 2016. "The Local Ceramic Wares of Philadelphia." Appendix C in *Archaeology of the City—The Museum of the American Revolution Site. Archaeological Data Recovery, Third and Chestnut Streets, Philadelphia Pennsylvania*, edited by Rebecca Yamin. Submitted to the Museum of the American Revolution. Commonwealth Heritage Group. On file at Independence National Historical Park Library, Philadelphia.

Glenn, Thomas A. 1891. "William Hudson, Mayor of Philadelphia, 1725–1726." *Pennsylvania Magazine of History and Biography* 15 (3): 336–343.

Goetz, Catherine. 1995. "A Woman of the 'Best Sort': The Diary of Elizabeth Drinker." In *Life in Early Philadelphia: Documents from the Revolutionary and Early National Periods*, edited by Billy G. Smith, 131–154. University Park: Pennsylvania State University Press.

Hechtlinger, Adelaide. 1970. *The Great Patent Medicine Era: Or, Without the Benefit of Doctor*. New York: Galahad.

Hunter, Robert and Juliette Gerhardt. 2016. An Eighteenth-Century American True-Porcelain Punch Bowl. In *Ceramics in America* 2016. Chipstone Foundation, Milwaukee, WI.

King, Moses. (1902) 2012. *Philadelphia and Notable Philadelphians*. New York: King. Digitization, New York: Columbia University Libraries.

Lehrman Institute. 2005–2017. "America's Founding Drama." http://lehrmaninstitute.org/history/founders.html.

Leone, Mark P. 2005. *The Archaeology of Liberty in an American Capital: Excavations in Annapolis*. Berkeley: University of California Press.

Little, Barbara J. 1992. "Explicit and Implicit Meaning in Material Culture and Print Culture." *Historical Archaeology* 26:85–94.

Mancl, Timothy. 2016. "The Lippincott Button Factory, 236–238 Ionic Street." In *Archaeology of the City—The Museum of the American Revolution Site. Archaeological Data Recovery, Third and Chestnut Streets, Philadelphia Pennsylvania*, edited by Rebecca Yamin, 150–160. Submitted to the Museum of the American Revolution. Commonwealth Heritage Group. On file at Independence National Historical Park Library, Philadelphia.

McMahon, A. Michael. 1992. "'Small Matters': Benjamin Franklin, Philadelphia, and the 'Progress of Cities.'" *Philadelphia Magazine of History and Biography* 116 (2): 158–179.

Mutual Assurance Company. 1832. Policy no. 5285. In the collections of the Historical Society of Pennsylvania, Philadelphia.

Noël-Hume, Ivor. 1969. *A Guide to Artifacts of Colonial America*. New York: Alfred A. Knopf.

Philadelphia County Deed Book. D33, 182–183. 1789. On file at the Recorder of Deeds, Philadelphia.

Philadelphia Yearly Meeting Minutes. Friends Historical Library. Swarthmore College. Swarthmore, PA

Ratini, Meagan. 2016. "The Jayne Building." In *Archaeology of the City—The Museum of the American Revolution Site. Archaeological Data Recovery, Third and Chestnut Streets, Philadelphia Pennsylvania*, edited by Rebecca Yamin, 128–149. Submitted to the Museum of the American Revolution. Commonwealth Heritage Group. On file at Independence National Historical Park Library, Philadelphia.

Richardson, Edgar P. 1982. "The Athens of America, 1800–1825." In *Philadelphia: A 300-Year History*, edited by Russell F. Weigley, 208–257. New York: W. W Norton.

Rorabaugh, W. J. 1979. *The Alcoholic Republic: An American Tradition*. New York: Oxford University Press.

Salinger, Sharon V. 2002. *Taverns and Drinking in Early America*. Baltimore: John Hopkins University Press.

Smith, Billy G. 1990. *The Lower Sort: Philadelphia's Laboring People 1750–1800*. Ithaca, NY: Cornell University Press.

Southwark Historical Society. 2014. "The Black Bear Tavern and Ball Alley." https://southwarkhistory.org/2014/.

Thompson, Peter. 1999. *Rum Punch and Revolution: Taverngoing and Public Life in Eighteenth-Century Philadelphia*. Philadelphia: University of Pennsylvania Press.

U.S. Quaker Meeting Records. https://www.swarthmore.edu/friends-historical-library/quaker-meeting-record/.

Wood, Gordon S. 1991. *The Radicalism of the American Revolution.* New York: Vintage.

Yamin, Rebecca. 1998. "Lurid Tales and Homely Stories of New York's Notorious Five Points." In *Archaeologists as Storytellers*, edited by Adrian Praetzellis and Mary Praetzellis. Special issue, *Historical Archaeology* 32(1):74–85.

———, ed. 2016. *Archaeology of the City—The Museum of the American Revolution Site. Archaeological Data Recovery, Third and Chestnut Streets, Philadelphia Pennsylvania.* Submitted to the Museum of the American Revolution. Commonwealth Heritage Group. On file at Independence National Historical Park Library, Philadelphia.

Yamin, Rebecca, Matthew D. Harris, Douglas C. McVarish, and Grace H. Ziesing. 2010. *Independence National Historical Park, Archeological Sensitivity Study (Phase IA Archeological Assessment), Independence Living History Center North Lot.* John Milner Associates, Inc. Prepared for and on file at Independence National Historical Park Library, Philadelphia.

Yamin, Rebecca, and Joseph Schuldenrein. 2007. "Landscape Archaeology in Lower Manhattan: The Collect Pond as an Evolving Cultural Landmark in New York City." In *Envisioning Landscape, Situations and Standpoints in Archaeology and Heritage*, edited by Dan Hicks, Laura McAtackney, and Graham Fairclough, 75–100. Walnut Creek, CA: Left Coast Press.

Young, James Harvey. 1961. *The Toadstool Millionaires: A Social History of Patent Medicines in America before Federal Regulation.* Princeton, NJ: Princeton University Press

INDEX